HAVE FAITH
IN
MASSACHUSETTS

Copyright, Notman

Calvin Coolidge

HAVE FAITH
IN
MASSACHUSETTS

A Collection of Speeches and Messages

BY

CALVIN COOLIDGE
Governor of Massachusetts

SECOND EDITION ENLARGED

BOSTON AND NEW YORK
HOUGHTON MIFFLIN COMPANY
The Riverside Press Cambridge

119975

INTRODUCTORY NOTE

THERE are certain fundamental principles of sound community life which cannot be stated too emphatically or too often. Few public men of to-day have shown a finer combination of right feeling and clear thinking about these principles, with a gift for the pithy expression of them, than has Governor Calvin Coolidge. It was an accurate phrase that President Meiklejohn used when, in conferring the degree of Doctor of Laws on him at Amherst College last June, he complimented him on teaching the lesson of "adequate brevity."

His speeches and messages abound in evidences of this gift, but in the main the speeches are not easily accessible. It has seemed to some of Governor Coolidge's admirers, as it has to the publishers of this little volume, that a real public service might be rendered by making a careful selection from the best of the speeches and issuing them in an attractive and convenient form. With his permission this has been done, and it is hoped that many readers will welcome the book in this time of special need of inspiring and steadying influences.

It is a time when all men should realize that, in the words of Governor Coolidge himself, "Laws must rest on the eternal foundations of righteousness"; that "Industry, thrift, character are not conferred by act or resolve. Government cannot relieve from toil." It is a time when we must "have faith in Massachusetts. We need a broader, firmer, deeper faith in the people, — a faith that men desire to do right, that the Commonwealth is founded upon a righteousness which will endure."

THE EDITORS

Boston, September, 1919

NOTE TO SECOND EDITION

In the issue of a second edition of this collection of Governor Coolidge's speeches and messages, the opportunity has been taken to add a proclamation and three recently delivered addresses, which bring the volume practically up to the date of publication.

Boston, October, 1919

The Commonwealth of Massachusetts.

By His Excellency

CALVIN COOLIDGE
GOVERNOR

A PROCLAMATION

Massachusetts has many glories. The last one she would wish to surrender is the glory of the men who have served her in war. While such devotion lives the Commonwealth is secure. Whatever dangers may threaten from within or without she can view them calmly. Turning to her veterans she can say "These are our defenders. They are invincible. In them is our safety."

War is the rule of force. Peace is the reign of law. When Massachusetts was settled the Pilgrims first dedicated themselves to a reign of law. When they set foot on Plymouth Rock they brought the Mayflower Compact, in which, calling on the Creator to witness, they agreed with each other to make just laws and render due submission and obedience. The date of that American document was written November 11, 1620.

After more than five years of the bitterest war in human experience, the last great stronghold of force, surrendering to the demands of America and her allies, agreed to cast aside the sword and live under the law. The date of that world document was written November 11, 1918.

Now, therefore, in grateful commemoration of the unsurpassed deeds of heroism performed by the service men of Massachusetts, of the sacrifice of her people, sometimes greater than life itself, of the service rendered by every war charity and organization, to honor those who bore arms, to recognize those who supported the government, in accordance with the law of the current year

TUESDAY, NOVEMBER 11, 1919

is set apart as a holiday for general observance and celebration of the home coming of Massachusetts soldiers, sailors and marines. In that welcome may we dedicate ourselves to a continued support of the cause for which they freely offered life, that there may be wiped away everywhere the burden of injustice and every attempt to rule by force, and that there may be ushered in a reign of law, that will ease the weak of their great burdens, and leave the strong, unhampered by the opposition of evil men, the opportunity to exert their whole energy for the welfare of their fellow men. Let war and all force end, and peace and all law reign.

GIVEN at the Executive Chamber, in Boston, this twenty-eighth day of October, in the year of our Lord one thousand nine hundred and nineteen, and of the Independence of the United States of America the one hundred and forty-fourth.

By His Excellency the Governor.

Calvin Coolidge

Albert P. Langley Secretary of the Commonwealth.

God Save the Commonwealth of Massachusetts.

CONTENTS

CONTENTS

HAVE FAITH
IN
MASSACHUSETTS

HAVE FAITH
IN
MASSACHUSETTS

I

TO THE STATE SENATE ON BEING ELECTED ITS PRESIDENT
JANUARY 7, 1914

HONORABLE SENATORS: — I thank you — with gratitude for the high honor given, with appreciation for the solemn obligations assumed — I thank you.

This Commonwealth is one. We are all members of one body. The welfare of the weakest and the welfare of the most powerful are inseparably bound together. Industry cannot flourish if labor languish. Transportation cannot prosper if manufactures decline. The general welfare cannot be provided for in any one act, but it is well to remember that the benefit of one is the benefit of all, and the neglect of one is the neglect of all. The suspension of one man's dividends is the suspension of another man's pay envelope.

Men do not make laws. They do but discover them. Laws must be justified by something more than the will of the majority. They must rest on the eternal foundation of righteousness. That state is most fortunate in its form of government which has the aptest instruments for the discovery of laws. The latest, most modern, and nearest perfect system that statesmanship has devised is representative government. Its weakness is the weakness of us imperfect human beings who administer it. Its strength is that even such administration secures to the people more blessings than any other system ever produced. No nation has discarded it and retained liberty. Representative government must be preserved.

Courts are established, not to determine the popularity of a cause, but to adjudicate and enforce rights. No litigant should be required to submit his case to the hazard and expense of a political campaign. No judge should be required to seek or receive political rewards. The courts of Massachusetts are known and honored wherever men love justice. Let their glory suffer no diminution at our hands. The electorate and judiciary cannot combine. A hearing means a hearing. When the trial of causes goes outside the court-room, Anglo-Saxon constitutional government ends.

The people cannot look to legislation generally for success. Industry, thrift, character, are not conferred by act or resolve. Government cannot relieve from toil. It can provide no substitute for the rewards of service. It can, of course, care for the defective and recognize distinguished merit. The normal must care for themselves. Self-government means self-support.

Man is born into the universe with a

personality that is his own. He has a right that is founded upon the constitution of the universe to have property that is his own. Ultimately, property rights and personal rights are the same thing. The one cannot be preserved if the other be violated. Each man is entitled to his rights and the rewards of his service be they never so large or never so small.

History reveals no civilized people among whom there were not a highly educated class, and large aggregations of wealth, represented usually by the clergy and the nobility. Inspiration has always come from above. Diffusion of learning has come down from the university to the common school — the kindergarten is last. No one would now expect to aid the common school by abolishing higher education.

It may be that the diffusion of wealth works in an analogous way. As the little red schoolhouse is builded in the college, it may be that the fostering and protection

of large aggregations of wealth are the only
foundation on which to build the prosperity of the whole people. Large profits
mean large pay rolls. But profits must be
the result of service performed. In no land
are there so many and such large aggregations of wealth as here; in no land do they
perform larger service; in no land will the
work of a day bring so large a reward in
material and spiritual welfare.

Have faith in Massachusetts. In some
unimportant detail some other States may
surpass her, but in the general results,
there is no place on earth where the people
secure, in a larger measure, the blessings of
organized government, and nowhere can
those functions more properly be termed
self-government.

Do the day's work. If it be to protect
the rights of the weak, whoever objects,
do it. If it be to help a powerful corpora-
tion better to serve the people, whatever
the opposition, do that. Expect to be

called a stand-patter, but don't be a stand-patter. Expect to be called a demagogue, but don't be a demagogue. Don't hesitate to be as revolutionary as science. Don't hesitate to be as reactionary as the multiplication table. Don't expect to build up the weak by pulling down the strong. Don't hurry to legislate. Give administration a chance to catch up with legislation.

We need a broader, firmer, deeper faith in the people — a faith that men desire to do right, that the Commonwealth is founded upon a righteousness which will endure, a reconstructed faith that the final approval of the people is given not to demagogues, slavishly pandering to their selfishness, merchandising with the clamor of the hour, but to statesmen, ministering to their welfare, representing their deep, silent, abiding convictions.

Statutes must appeal to more than material welfare. Wages won't satisfy, be they never so large. Nor houses; nor lands;

nor coupons, though they fall thick as the leaves of autumn. Man has a spiritual nature. Touch it, and it must respond as the magnet responds to the pole. To that, not to selfishness, let the laws of the Commonwealth appeal. Recognize the immortal worth and dignity of man. Let the laws of Massachusetts proclaim to her humblest citizen, performing the most menial task, the recognition of his manhood, the recognition that all men are peers, the humblest with the most exalted, the recognition that all work is glorified. Such is the path to equality before the law. Such is the foundation of liberty under the law. Such is the sublime revelation of man's relation to man — Democracy.

II

AMHERST COLLEGE ALUMNI ASSOCIA-
TION, BOSTON

FEBRUARY 4, 1916

WE live in an age which questions everything. The past generation was one of religious criticism. This is one of commercial
criticism.

We have seen the development of great
industries. It has been represented that
some of these have not been free from
blame. In this development some men have
seemed to prosper beyond the measure of
their service, while others have appeared
to be bound to toil beyond their strength
for less than a decent livelihood.

As a result of criticising these conditions
there has grown up a too well-developed
public opinion along two lines; one, that
the men engaged in great affairs are selfish and greedy and not to be trusted,

that business activity is not moral and the whole system is to be condemned; and the other, that employment, that work, is a curse to man, and that working hours ought to be as short as possible or in some way abolished. After criticism, our religious faith emerged clearer and stronger and freed from doubt. So will our business relations emerge, purified but justified.

The evidence of evolution and the facts of history tell us of the progress and development of man through various steps and ages, known by various names. We learn of the stone age, the bronze, and the iron age. We can see the different steps in the growth of the forms of government; how anarchy was put down by the strong arm of the despot, of the growth of aristocracy, of limited monarchies and of parliaments, and finally democracy.

But in all these changes man took but one step at a time. Where we can trace history, no race ever stepped directly from the stone age to the iron age and no nation ever passed directly from depotism to democracy. Each advance has been made only when a previous stage was approaching perfection, even to conditions which are now sometimes lost arts.

We have reached the age of invention, of commerce, of great industrial enterprise. It is often referred to as selfish and materialistic.

Our economic system has been attacked from above and from below. But the short answer lies in the teachings of history. The hope of a Watt or an Edison lay in the men who chipped flint to perfection. The seed of democracy lay in a perfected despotism. The hope of to-morrow lies in the development of the instruments of to-day. The prospect of advance lies in maintaining those conditions which have stimulated invention and industry and commerce. The only road to a more progressive age lies in perfecting the instrumentalities of this age.

The only hope for peace lies in the perfection of the arts of war.

"We build the ladder by which we rise
.   .   .   .
And we mount to the summit round by round."

All growth depends upon activity. Life is manifest only by action. There is no development physically or intellectually without effort, and effort means work. Work is not a curse, it is the prerogative of intelligence, the only means to manhood, and the measure of civilization. Savages do not work. The growth of a sentiment that despises work is an appeal from civilization to barbarism.

I would not be understood as making a sweeping criticism of current legislation along these lines. I, too, rejoice that an awakened conscience has outlawed commercial standards that were false or low and that an awakened humanity has decreed that the working and living condition of our citizens must be worthy of true manhood and true womanhood.

I agree that the measure of success is not merchandise but character. But I do criticise those sentiments, held in all too respectable quarters, that our economic system is fundamentally wrong, that commerce is only selfishness, and that our citizens, holding the hope of all that America means, are living in industrial slavery. I appeal to Amherst men to reiterate and sustain the Amherst doctrine, that the man who builds a factory builds a temple, that the man who works there worships there, and to each is due, not scorn and blame, but reverence and praise.

III

BROCKTON CHAMBER OF COMMERCE
APRIL 11, 1916

MAN'S nature drives him ever onward. He is forever seeking development. At one time it may be by the chase, at another by warfare, and again by the quiet arts of peace and commerce, but something within is ever calling him on to "replenish the earth and subdue it."

It may be of little importance to determine at any time just where we are, but it is of the utmost importance to determine whither we are going. Set the course aright and time must bring mankind to the ultimate goal.

We are living in a commercial age. It is often designated as selfish and materialistic. We are told that everything has been commercialized. They say it has not been enough that this spirit should dominate

the marts of trade, it has spread to every
avenue of human endeavor, to our arts,
cur sciences and professions, our politics,
our educational institutions and even into
the pulpit; and because of this there are
those who have gone so far in their criticism of commercialism as to advocate the
destruction of all enterprise and the aboli-
tion of all property.

Destructive criticism is always easy because, despite some campaign oratory,
some of us are not yet perfect. But constructive criticism is not so easy. The
faults of commercialism, like many other
faults, lie in the use we make of it. Before
we decide upon a wholesale condemnation
of the most noteworthy spirit of modern
times it would be well to examine carefully
what that spirit has done to advance the
welfare of mankind.

Wherever we can read human history,
the answer is always the same. Where commerce has flourished there civilization has

increased. It has not sufficed that men should tend their flocks, and maintain themselves in comfort on their industry alone, however great. It is only when the exchange of products begins that development follows. This was the case in ancient Babylon, whose records of trade and banking we are just beginning to read. Their merchandise went by canal and caravan to the ends of the earth. It was not the war galleys, but the merchant vessel of Phœnicia, of Tyre, and Carthage that brought them civilization and power. To-day it is not the battle fleet, but the mercantile marine which in the end will determine the destiny of nations. The advance of our own land has been due to our trade, and the comfort and happiness of our people are dependent on our general business conditions. It is only a figure of poetry that "wealth accumulates and men decay." Where wealth has accumulated, there the arts and sciences have

flourished, there education has been diffused, and of contemplation liberty has
been born. The progress of man has been
measured by his commercial prosperity. I
believe that these considerations are sufficient to justify our business enterprise and
activity, but there are still deeper reasons.

I have intended to indicate not only
that commerce is an instrument of great
power, but that commercial development
is necessary to all human progress. What,
then, of the prevalent criticism? Men have
mistaken the means for the end. It is not
enough for the individual or the nation to
acquire riches. Money will not purchase
character or good government. We are
under the injunction to "replenish the
earth and subdue it," not so much because
of the help a new earth will be to us, as because by that process man is to find himself and thereby realize his highest destiny.
Men must work for more than wages, factories must turn out more than merchan-

dise, or there is naught but black despair ahead.

If material rewards be the only measure of success, there is no hope of a peaceful solution of our social questions, for they will never be large enough to satisfy. But such is not the case. Men struggle for material success because that is the path, the process, to the development of character. We ought to demand economic justice, but most of all because it is justice. We must forever realize that material rewards are limited and in a sense they are only incidental, but the development of character is unlimited and is the only essential. The measure of success is not the quantity of merchandise, but the quality of manhood which is produced.

These, then, are the justifying conceptions of the spirit of our age; that commerce is the foundation of human progress and prosperity and the great artisan of human character. Let us dismiss the general indictment that has all too long hung over business enterprise. While we continue to condemn, unsparingly, selfishness and greed and all trafficking in the natural rights of man, let us not forget to respect thrift and industry and enterprise. Let us look to the service rather than to the reward. Then shall we see in our industrial army, from the most exalted captain to the humblest soldier in the ranks, a purpose worthy to minister to the highest needs of man and to fulfil the hope of a fairer day.

IV

AT THE HOME OF DANIEL WEBSTER
MARSHFIELD
JULY 4, 1916

HISTORY is revelation. It is the manifesta-
tion in human affairs of a "power not ourselves that makes for righteousness." Savages have no history. It is the mark of
civilization. This New England of ours
slumbered from the dawn of creation until
the beginning of the seventeenth century,
not unpeopled, but with no record of human events worthy of a name. Different
races came, and lived, and vanished, but
the story of their existence has little more
of interest for us than the story the natural-
ist tells of the animal kingdom, or the geol-
ogist relates of the formation of the crust
of the earth. It takes men of larger vision
and higher inspiration, with a power to im-
part a larger vision and a higher inspira-

tion to the people, to make history. It is
not a negative, but a positive achievement.
It is unconcerned with idolatry or despotism or treason or rebellion or betrayal, but
bows in reverence before Moses or Hampden or Washington or Lincoln or the
Light that shone on Calvary.

July 4, 1776, was a day of history in its
high and true significance. Not because the
underlying principles set out in the Declaration of Independence were new; they
are older than the Christian religion, or
Greek philosophy, nor was it because history is made by proclamation or declaration; history is made only by action. But
it was an historic day because the representatives of three millions of people there
vocalized Concord and Lexington and
Bunker Hill, which gave notice to the
world that they were acting, and proposed
to act, and to found an independent nation, on the theory that "all men are
created equal; that they are endowed

by their Creator with certain inalienable rights; that among these are life, liberty, and the pursuit of happiness." The wonder and glory of the American people is not the ringing declaration of that day, but the action, then already begun, and in the process of being carried out in spite of every obstacle that war could interpose, making the theory of freedom and equality a reality. We revere that day because it marks the beginnings of independence, the beginnings of a constitution that was finally to give universal freedom and equality to all American citizens, the beginnings of a government that was to recognize beyond all others the power and worth and dignity of man. There began the first of governments to acknowledge that it was founded on the sovereignty of the people. There the world first beheld the revelation of modern democracy.

Democracy is not a tearing-down; it is a building-up. It is not a denial of the divine right of kings; it supplements that claim with the assertion of the divine right of all men. It does not destroy; it fulfils. It is the consummation of all theories of government; to the spirit of which all the nations of the earth must yield. It is the great constructive force of the ages. It is the alpha and omega of man's relation to man, the beginning and the end. There is and can be no more doubt of the triumph of democracy in human affairs, than there is of the triumph of gravitation in the physical world; the only question is how and when. Its foundation lays hold upon eternity.

These are some of the ideals that the founders of our institutions expressed, in part unconsciously, on that momentous day now passed by one hundred and forty years. They knew that ideals do not maintain themselves. They knew that they there declared a purpose which would be resisted by the forces, on land and sea, of the mightiest empire of the earth. Without the resolution of the people of the Colonies to resort to arms, and without the guiding military genius of Washington, the Declaration of Independence would be naught in history but the vision of doctrinaires, a mockery of sounding brass and tinkling cymbal. Let us never forget that it was that resolution and that genius which made it the vitalizing force of a great nation. It takes service and sacrifice to maintain ideals.

But it is far more than the Declaration of Independence that brings us here to-day. That was, indeed, a great document. It was drawn up by Thomas Jefferson when he was at his best. It was the product of men who seemed inspired. No greater company ever assembled to interpret the voice of the people or direct the destinies of a nation. The events of history may have added to it, but subtracted nothing. Wisdom and experience have increased the admiration of it. Time and critcism have not shaken it. It stands with ordinance and law, charter and constitution, prophecy and revelation, whether we read them in the history of Babylon, the results of Runnymede, the Ten Commandments, or the Sermon on the Mount. But, however worthy of our reverence and admiration, however preëminent, it was only one incident of a great forward movement of the human race, of which the American Revolution was itself only a larger incident. It was not so much a struggle of the Colonies against the tyranny of bad government, as against wrong principles of government, and for self-government. It was man realizing himself. It was sovereignty from within which responded to the alarm of Paul Revere on that April night, and which went marching, gun in hand, against sovereignty from without, wherever it was found on earth. It only paused at Concord, or Yorktown, then marched on to Paris, to London, to Moscow, to Pekin. Against it the powers of privilege and the forces of despotism could not prevail. Superstition and sham cannot stand before intelligence and reality. The light that first broke over the thirteen Colonies lying along the Atlantic Coast was destined to illuminate the world. It has been a struggle against the forces of darkness; victory has been and is still delayed in some quarters, but the result is not in doubt. All the forces of the universe are ranged on the side of democracy. It must prevail.

In the train of this idea there has come to man a long line of collateral blessings. Freedom has many sides and angles. Human slavery has been swept away. With security of personal rights has come security of property rights. The freedom of the human mind is recognized in the right of free speech and free press. The public schools have made education possible for all, and ignorance a disgrace. A most significant development of respect for man has come to be respect for his occupation. It is not alone for the learned professions that great treasures are now poured out. Technical, trade, and vocational schools for teaching skill in occupations are fostered and nourished, with the same care as colleges and universities for the teaching of sciences and the classics. Democracy not only ennobled man; it has ennobled industry. In political affairs the vote of the humblest has long counted for as much as the vote of the most exalted. We are working towards the day when, in our industrial life, equal honor shall fall to equal endeavor, whether it be exhibited in the office or in the shop.

These are some of the results of that great world movement, which, first exhibiting itself in the Continental Congress of America, carried her arms to victory, through the sacrifice of a seven years' revolutionary war, and wrote into the Treaty of Paris the recognition of the right of the people to rule: since which days existence on this planet has had a new meaning; a result which, changing the old order of things, putting the race under the control and guidance of new forces, rescued man from every thraldom, but laid on him every duty.

We know that only ignorance and superstition seek to explain events by fate and destiny, yet there is a fascination in such speculations born, perhaps, of human frailty. How happens it that James Otis laid out in 1762 the then almost treasonable proposition that "Kings were made for the good of the people, and not the people for them," in a pamphlet which was circulated among the Colonists? What school had taught Patrick Henry that national outlook which he expressed in the opening debates of the first Continental Congress when he said, "I am not a Virginian, but an American," and which hurried him on to the later cry of "Liberty or death?" How

was it that the filling of a vacancy sent
Thomas Jefferson to the second Continental
Congress, there to pen the immortal Declaration we this day celebrate? No other
living man could have excelled him in preparation for, or in the execution of, that
great task. What circumstance put the
young George Washington under the military instruction of a former army officer,
and then gave him years of training to lead
the Continental forces? What settled Ethan
Allen in the wilderness of the Green Moun-
tains ready to strike Ticonderoga? Whence
came that power to draft state papers, in a
new and unlettered land, which compelled
the admiration of the cultured Earl of
Chatham? What lengthened out the days
of Benjamin Franklin that he might negotiate the Treaty of Paris? What influence
sent the miraculous voice of Daniel Webster from the outlying settlements of New
Hampshire to rouse the land with his appeal for Liberty and Union? And finally

who raised up Lincoln, to lead, to inspire, and to die, that the opening assertion of the Declaration might stand at last fulfilled?

These thoughts are overpowering. But let us beware of fate and destiny. Barbarians have decreased, but barbarism still exists. Rome boasted the name of the Eternal City. It was but eight hundred years from the sack of the city by one tribe of barbarians to the sack of the city by another tribe of barbarians. Between lay something akin to a democratic commonwealth. Then games, and bribes for the populace, with dictators and Cæsars, while later the Prætorian Guard sold the royal purple to the highest bidder. After which came Alaric, the Goth, and night. Since when democracy lay dormant for some fifteen centuries. We may claim with reason that our Nation has had the guidance of Providence; we may know that our form of government must ultimately prevail upon earth; but what guaranty have we that it shall be maintained here? What proof that some unlineal hand, some barbarism, without or within, shall not wrench the sceptre of democracy from our grasp? The rule of princes, the privilege of birth, has come down through the ages; the rule of the people has not yet marked a century and a half. There is no absolute proof, no positive guaranty, but there is hope and high expectation, and the path is not uncharted.

It may be some help to know that, however much of glory, there is no magic in American democracy. Let us examine some more of this Declaration of ours, and examine it in the light of the events of those solemn days in which it was adopted.

Men of every clime have lavished much admiration upon the first part of the Declaration of Independence, and rightly so, for it marked the entry of new forces and new ideals into human affairs. Its admirers have sometimes failed in their attempts to live by it, but none have successfully disputed its truth. It is the realization of the true glory and worth of man, which, when once admitted, wrought vast changes that have marked all history since its day. All this relates to natural rights, fascinating to dwell upon, but not sufficient to live by. The signers knew that well; more important still, the people whom they represented knew it. So they did not stop there. After asserting that man was to stand out in the universe with a new and supreme importance, and that governments were instituted to insure life, liberty, and the pursuit of happiness, they did not shrink from the logical conclusion of this doctrine. They knew that the duty between the citizen and the State was reciprocal. They knew that the State called on its citizens for their property and their lives; they laid down the proposition that government was to protect the citizen in his life, liberty, and pursuit of happiness. At some expense? Yes. Those prudent and thrifty men had no false notions about incurring expense. They knew the value of increasing their material resources, but they knew that prosperity was a means, not an end. At cost of life? Yes. These sons of the Puritans, of the Huguenots, of the men of Londonderry, braved exile to secure peace, but they were not afraid to die in defence of their convictions. They put no limit on what the State must do for the citizen in his hour of need. While they required all, they gave all. Let us read their conclusion in their own words, and mark its simplicity and majesty: "And for the support of this Declaration, with a firm reliance on the protection of Divine Providence, we mutually pledge to each other our lives, our fortunes, and our sacred honor." There is no cringing reservation here, no alternative, and no delay. Here is the voice of the plain men of Middlesex, promising Yorktown, promising Appomattox.

The doctrine of the Declaration of In-

dependence, predicated upon the glory of
man, and the corresponding duty of society, is that the rights of citizens are to be
protected with every power and resource
of the State, and a government that does
any less is false to the teachings of that
great document, of the name American.
Beyond this, the principle that it is the obligation of the people to rise and overthrow
government which fails in these respects.
But above all, the call to duty, the pledge
of fortune and of life, nobility of character
through nobility of action: this is Americanism.

"Woe for us if we forget, we that hold by these."

Herein are the teachings of this day —
touching the heights of man's glory and the
depths of man's duty. Here lies the path to
national preservation, and there is no other.
Education, the progress of science, commercial prosperity, yes, and peace, all these and
their accompanying blessings are worthy
and commendable objects of attainment.

But these are not the end, whether these come or no; the end lies in action — action in accord with the eternal principles of the Declaration of Independence; the words of the Continental Congress, but the deeds of the Army of the Revolution.

This is the meaning of America. And it is all our own. Doctrinaires and visionaries may shudder at it. The privilege of birth may jeer at it. The practical politician may scoff at it. But the people of the Nation respond to it, and march away to Mexico to the rescue of a colored trooper as they marched of old to the rescue of an emperor. The assertion of human rights is naught but a call to human sacrifice. This is yet the spirit of the American people. Only so long as this flame burns shall we endure and the light of liberty be shed over the nations of the earth. May the increase of the years increase for America only the devotion to this spirit, only the intensity of this flame, and the eternal truth of Lowell's lines:

" What were our lives without thee?
  What all our lives to save thee?
  We reck not what we gave thee;
  We will not dare to doubt thee,
  But ask whatever else and we will **dare.**"

V

RIVERSIDE

AUGUST 28, 1916

IT may be that there would be votes for the Republican Party in the promise of low taxes and vanishing expenditures. I can see an opportunity for its candidates to pose as the apostles of retrenchment and reform. I am not one of those who believe votes are to be won by misrepresentations, skilful presentations of half truths, and plausible deductions from false premises. Good government cannot be found on the bargain-counter. We have seen samples of bargain-counter government in the past when low tax rates were secured by increasing the bonded debt for current expenses or refusing to keep our institutions up to the standard in repairs, extensions, equipment, and accommodations. I refuse, and the Republican Party refuses, to endorse that method

of sham and shoddy economy. New proj-
ects can wait, but the commitments of the
Commonwealth must be maintained. We
cannot curtail the usual appropriations or
the care of mothers with dependent children or the support of the poor, the insane,
and the infirm. The Democratic programme
of cutting the State tax, by vetoing appropriations of the utmost urgency for im-
provements and maintenance costs of institutions and asylums of the unfortunates
of the State, cannot be the example for a
Republican administration. The result has
been that our institutions are deficient in
resources — even in sleeping accommodations — and it will take years to restore
them to the old-time Republican efficiency.
Our party will have no part in a scheme of
economy which adds to the misery of the
wards of the Commonwealth — the sick,
the insane, and the unfortunate; those who
are too weak even to protest.

Because I know these conditions I know

a Republican administration would face an increasing State tax rather than not see them remedied.

The Republican Party lit the fire of progress in Massachusetts. It has tended it faithfully. It will not flicker now. It has provided here conditions of employment, and safeguards for health, that are surpassed nowhere on earth. There will be no backward step. The reuniting of the Republican Party means no reaction in the protection of women and children in our industrial life. These laws are settled. These principles are established. Minor modifications are possible, but the foundations are not to be disturbed. The advance may have been too rapid in some cases, but there can be no retreat. That is the position of the great majority of those who constitute our party.

We recognize there is need of relief — need to our industries, need to our population in manufacturing centres; but it must come from construction, not from destruction. Put an administration on Beacon Hill that can conserve our resources, that can protect us from further injuries, until a national Republican policy can restore those conditions of confidence and prosperity under which our advance began and under which it can be resumed.

This makes the coming State election take on a most important aspect — not that it can furnish all the needed relief, but that it will increase the probability of a complete relief in the near future if it be crowned with Republican victory.

VI

AT THE HOME OF AUGUSTUS P. GARDNER, HAMILTON
September, 1916

Standing here in the presence of our host, our thoughts naturally turn to a discussion of "Preparedness." I do not propose to overlook that issue; but I shall offer suggestions of another kind of "preparedness." Not that I shrink from full and free consideration of the military needs of our country. Nor do I agree that it is now necessary to remain silent regarding the domestic or foreign relations of this Nation.

I agree that partisanship should stop at the boundary line, but I assert that patriotism should begin there. Others, however, have covered this field, and I leave it to them and to you.

I do, however, propose to discuss the "preparedness" of the State to care for its unfortunates. And I propose to do this without any party bias and without blame upon any particular individual, but in just criticism of a system.

In Massachusetts, we are citizens before we are partisans. The good name of the Commonwealth is of more moment to us than party success. But unfortunately, because of existing conditions, that good name, in one particular at least, is now in jeopardy.

Massachusetts, for twenty years, has been able honestly to boast of the care it has bestowed upon her sick, poor, and insane. Her institutions have been regarded as models throughout the world. We are falling from that proud estate; crowded housing conditions, corridors used for sleeping purposes, are not only not unusual, but are coming to be the accepted standard. The heads of asylums complain that maintenance and the allowance for food supply and supervision are being skimped.

On August 1 of this year, the institutions throughout the State housed more than 700 patients above what they were designed to accommodate, and I am told the crowding is steadily increasing. That is one reason I have been at pains to set forth that I do not see the way clear to make a radical reduction in the annual State budget. I now repeat that declaration, in spite of contradiction, because I know the citizens of this State have no desire for economies gained at such a sacrifice. The people have no stomach for retrenchment of that sort.

A charge of overcrowding, which must mean a lack of care, is not to be carelessly made. You are entitled to facts, as well as phrases. I gave the whole number now confined in our institutions above the stated capacity as over 700. About August 1, Danvers had 1530 in an institution of 1350 capacity. Northampton, my home town, had 913, in a hospital built for 819. In Boston State Hospital, there were 1572, where the capacity was 1406. Westboro had 1260 inmates, with capacity for 1161, and Medfield had 1615, where the capacity was 1542. These capacities are given from official recorded accommodations.

This was not the practice of the past, and there can be no question as to where the responsibility rests. The General Court has done its best, but there has been a halt elsewhere. A substantial appropriation was made for a new State Hospital for the Metropolitan District, and an additional appropriation for a new institution for the feeble-minded in the western part of the State. In its desire to hasten matters, the legislature went even further and granted money for plans for a new hospital in the Metropolitan District, to relieve part of the outside congestion, but the needed relief is still in the future.

I feel the time has come when the people must assert themselves and show that they will tolerate no delay and no parsimony in the care of our unfortunates. Restore the fame of our State in the handling of these problems to its former lustre.

I repeat that this is not partisan. I am not criticising individuals. I am denouncing a system. When you substitute patronage for patriotism, administration breaks down. We need more of the Office Desk and less of the Show Window in politics. Let men in office substitute the midnight oil for the limelight. Let Massachusetts return to the sound business methods which were exemplified in the past by such Democrats in the East as Governor Gaston and Governor Douglas, and by such Republicans in the West as Governor Robinson and Governor Crane.

Above all, let us not, in our haste to prepare for war, forget to prepare for peace. The issue is with you. You can, by your votes, show what system you stamp with the approval of enlightened Massachusetts Public Opinion.

VII

LAFAYETTE BANQUET, FALL RIVER
September 4, 1916

SEEMINGLY trifling events oft carry in their train great consequences. The firing of a gun in the backwoods of Pennsylvania, Macaulay tells us, started the Seven Years' War which set the world in conflagration, causing men to fight each other on every shore of the seven seas and giving new masters to the most ancient of empires. We see to-day fifteen nations engaged in the most terrific war in the history of the human race and trace its origin to the bullet of a madman fired in the Balkans. It is true that the flintlock gun at Lexington was not the first, nor yet the last, to fire a "shot heard round the world." It was not the distance it travelled, but the message it carried which has marked it out above all other human events. It was the character of that message which claimed the attention of him we this day honor, in the far-off fortress of the now famous Metz; it was because it roused in the listener a sympathetic response that it was destined to link forever the events of Concord and Lexington and Bunker Hill and Dorchester Heights, in our Commonwealth, with the name of Lafayette.

For there was a new tone in those Massachusetts guns. It was not the old lust of conquest, not the sullen roar of hatred and revenge, but a higher, clearer note of a people asserting their inalienable sovereignty. It is a happy circumstance that one of our native-born, Benjamin Franklin, was instrumental in bringing Lafayette to America; but beyond that it is fitting at this time to give a thought to our Commonwealth because his ideals, his character, his life, were all in sympathy with that great Revolution which was begun within her borders and carried to a successful con-

clusion by the sacrifice of her treasure and
her blood. It was not the able legal argument of James Otis against the British
Writs of Assistance, nor the petitions and
remonstrances of the Colonists to the British throne, admirable though they were,
that aroused the approbation and brought
his support to our cause. It was not alone
that he agreed with the convictions of the
Continental Congress. He saw in the example of Massachusetts a people who would
shrink from no sacrifice to defend rights
which were beyond price. It was not the
Tories, fleeing to Canada, that attracted
him. It was the patriots, bearing arms,
and he brought them not a pen but a sword.
"Resistance to tyranny is obedience to
law," and "obedience to law is liberty."
Those are the foundations of the Commonwealth. It was these principles in action
which appealed to that young captain of
dragoons and brought the sword and resources of the aristocrat to battle for de-

mocracy. I love to think of his connection with our history. I love to think of him at the dedication of the Bunker Hill Monument receiving the approbation of the Nation from the lips of Daniel Webster. I love to think of the long line of American citizens of French blood in our Commonwealth to-day, ready to defend the principles he fought for, "Liberty under the Law," citizens who, like him, look not with apology, but with respect and approval and admiration on that sentiment inscribed on the white flag of Massachusetts, *"Ense petit placidam sub libertate quietem"* (With a sword she seeks secure peace under liberty).

VIII

NORFOLK REPUBLICAN CLUB, BOSTON
OCTOBER 9, 1916

LAST night at Somerville I spoke on some of the fundamental differences between the Republican and Democratic policies, and showed how we were dependent on Republican principles as a foundation on which to erect any advance in our social and economic welfare.

This year the Republican Party has adopted a very advanced platform. That was natural, for we have always been the party of progress, and have given our attention to that, when we were not engaged in a life-and-death struggle to overcome the fallacies put forth by our opponents, with which we are all so familiar. The result has been that here in Massachusetts, where our party has ever been strong, and where we have framed legislation for more than fifty years, more progress has been made along the lines of humanitarian legislation than in any other State. We have felt free to call on our industries to make large outlays along these lines because we have furnished them with the advantages of a protective tariff and an honest and efficient state government. The consequences have been that in this State the hours and conditions of labor have been better than anywhere else on earth. Those provisions for safety, sanitation, compensations for accidents, and for good living conditions have now been almost entirely worked out. There remains, however, the condition of sickness, age, misfortune, lack of employment, or some other cause, that temporarily renders people unable to care for themselves. Our platform has taken up this condition.

We have long been familiar with insurance to cover losses. You will readily recall the different kinds. Formerly it was only used in commerce, by the well-to-do. Recently it has been adapted to the use of all our people by the great industrial companies which have been very successful. Our State has adopted a system of savings-bank insurance, thus reducing the expense. Now, social insurance will not be, under a Republican interpretation, any new form of outdoor relief, some new scheme of living on the town. It will be an extension of the old familiar principle to the needs at hand, and so popularized as to meet the requirements of our times.

It ought to be understood, however, that there can be no remedy for lack of industry and thrift, secured by law. It ought to be understood that no scheme of insurance and no scheme of government aid is likely to make us all prosperous. And above all, these remedies must go forward on the firm foundation of an independent, self-supporting, self-governing people. But we do honestly put forward a proposition for the relief of misfortune.

The Republican Party is proposing humanitarian legislation to build up character, to establish independence, not pauperism; it will in the future, as in the past, ever stand opposed to the establishment of one class who shall live on the Government, and another class who shall pay the taxes. To those who fear we are turning Socialists, and to those who think we are withholding just and desirable public aid and support, I say that government under the Republican Party will continue in the future to be so administered as to breed not mendicants, but men. Humanitarian legislation is going to be the handmaid of character.

IX

PUBLIC MEETING ON THE HIGH COST OF LIVING, FANEUIL HALL
DECEMBER 9, 1916

THE great aim of American institutions is the protection of the individual. That is the principle which lies at the foundation of Anglo-Saxon liberty. It matters not with what power the individual is assailed, nor whether that power is represented by wealth or place or numbers; against it the humblest American citizen has the right to the protection of his Government by every force that Government can command.

This right would be but half expressed if it ran only to a remedy after a wrong is inflicted; it should and does run to the prevention of a wrong which is threatened. We find our citizens, to-day, not so much suffering from the high cost of living, though that is grievous enough, as threatened with an increasing cost which will bring suffering and misery to a large body of our inhabitants. So we come here not only to discuss providing a remedy for what is now existing, but some protection to ward off what is threatening to be a worse calamity. We shall utterly fail of our purpose to provide relief unless we look at things as they are. It is useless to indulge in indiscriminate abuse. We must not confuse the innocent with the guilty; it must be our object to allay suspicion, not to create it. The great body of our tradespeople are honest and conscientious, anxious to serve their customers for a fair return for their service. We want their coöperation in our pursuit of facts; we want to coöperate with them in proposing and securing a remedy. We do not deny the existence of economic laws, nor the right to profit by a change of conditions.

But we do claim the right and duty of the Government to investigate and punish any artificial creation of high prices by means of illegal monopolies or restraints of trade. And above all, we claim the right of publicity. That is a remedy with an arm longer and stronger than that of the law. Let us know what is going on and the remedy will provide itself. In working along this line we shall have great help from the newspapers. The American people are prepared to meet any reasonable burden; they are not asking for charity or favor; fair prices and fair profits they will gladly pay; but they demand information that they are fair, and an immediate reduction if they are not.

The Commonwealth has just provided money for an investigation by a competent commission. Its Police Department, its Law Department, are also at the service of our citizens. Let us refrain from suspicion; let us refrain from all indiscriminate blame; but let us present at once to the proper authorities all facts and all evidence of unfair practices. Let all our merchants, of whatever degree, assist in this work for the public good and let the individual see and feel that all his rights are protected by his Government.

X

ONE HUNDREDTH ANNIVERSARY DINNER OF THE PROVIDENT INSTITUTION FOR SAVINGS

DECEMBER 13, 1916

THE history of the institution we here celebrate reaches back more than one third of the way to the landing of the Mayflower — back to the day of the men who signed the Declaration of Independence, who saw Prescott, Pomeroy, Stark, and Warren at Bunker Hill, who followed Washington and his generals from Dochester Heights to Yorktown, and saw the old Bay Colony become the Commonwealth of Massachusetts. They had seen a nation in the making. They founded their government on the rights of the individual. They had no hesitation in defending those rights against the invasion of a British King and Parliament, by a Revolutionary War, nor in criticising their own Government at Washington when they thought an invasion of those rights was again threatened by the preliminaries and the prosecution of the War of 1812. They had made the Commonwealth. They understood its Government. They knew it was a part of themselves, their own organization. They had not acquired the state of mind that enabled them to stand aloof and regard government as something apart and separate from the people. It would never have occurred to them that they could not transact for themselves any other business just as well as they could transact for themselves the business of government. They were the men who had fought a war to limit the power of government and enlarge the privileges of the individual.

It was the same spirit that made Massachusetts that made the Provident Institution for Savings. What the men of that day wanted they made for themselves. They would never have thought of asking Congress to keep their money in the post-office. They did not want their commercial privileges interfered with by having the Government buy and sell for them. They had the self-reliance and the independence to prefer to do those things for themselves. This is the spirit that founded Massachusetts, the spirit that has seen your bank grow until it could now probably purchase all there was of property in the Commonwealth when it began its existence. I want to see that spirit still preëminent here. I want to see a deeper realization on the part of the people that this is their Commonwealth, their Government; that they control it, that they pay its expenses, that it is, after all, only a part of themselves; that any attempt to shift upon it their duties, their responsibilities, or their support will in the end only delude, degrade, impoverish, and enslave. Your institution points the only way, through self-control, self-denial, and self-support, to self-government, to independence, to a more generous liberty, and to a firmer establishment of individual rights.

XI

ASSOCIATED INDUSTRIES DINNER
BOSTON
DECEMBER 15, 1916

DURING the past few years we have questioned the soundness of many principles that had for a long time been taken for granted. We have examined the foundations of our institutions of government. We have debated again the theories of the men who wrote the Declaration of Independence, the Constitution of the Nation, and laid down the fundamental law of our own Commonwealth. Along with this examination of our form of government has gone an examination of our social, industrial, and economic system. What is to come out of it all?

In the last fifty years we have had a material prosperity in this country the like of which was never beheld before. A prosperity which not only built up great industries, great transportation systems, great banks and a great commerce, but a prosperity under whose influence arts and sciences, education and charity flourished most abundantly. It was little wonder that men came to think that prosperity was the chief end of man and grew arrogant in the use of its power. It was little wonder that such a misunderstanding arose that one part of the community thought the owners and managers of our great industries were robbers, or that they thought some of the people meant to confiscate all property. It has been a costly investigation, but if we can arrive at a better understanding of our economic and social laws it will be worth all it cost.

As a part of this discussion we have had many attempts at regulation of industrial activity by law. Some of it has proceeded on the theory that if those who enjoyed material prosperity used it for wrong purposes, such prosperity should be limited or abolished.   That is as sound as it would be to abolish writing to prevent forgery. We need to keep forever in mind that guilt is personal; if there is to be punishment let it fall on the evil-doer, let us not condemn the instrument. We need power. Is the steam engine too strong? Is electricity too swift? Can any prosperity be too great? Can any instrument of commerce or industry ever be too powerful to serve the public needs? What then of the anti-trust laws? They are sound in theory. Their assemblances of wealth are broken up because they were assembled for an unlawful purpose. It is the purpose that is condemned. You men who represent our industries can see that there is the same right to disperse unlawful assembling of wealth or power that there is to disperse a mob that has met to lynch or riot. But that principle does not denounce town-meetings or prayer-meetings.

We have established here a democracy on the principle that all men are created equal.

It is our endeavor to extend equal blessings to all. It can be done approximately if we establish the correct standards. We are coming to see that we are dependent upon commercial and industrial prosperity, not only for the creation of wealth, but for the solving of the great problem of the distribution of wealth. There is just one condition on which men can secure employment and a living, nourishing, profitable wage, for whatever they contribute to the enterprise, be it labor or capital, and that condition is that some one make a profit by it. That is the sound basis for the distribution of wealth and the only one. It cannot be done by law, it cannot be done by public ownership, it cannot be done by socialism. When you deny the right to a profit you deny the right of a reward to thrift and industry.

The scientists tell us that the same force that rounds the teardrop moulds the earth. Physical laws have their analogy in social and industrial life. The law that builds up the people is the law that builds up industry. What price could the millions, who have found the inestimable blessings of American citizenship around our great industrial centres, after coming here from lands of oppression, afford to pay to those who organized those industries? Shall we not recognize the great service they have done the cause of humanity? Have we not seen what happens to industry, to transportation, to all commercial activity which we call business when profit fails? Have we not seen the suffering and misery which it entails upon the people?

Let us recognize the source of these fundamental principles and not hesitate to assert them. Let us frown upon greed and selfishness, but let us also condemn envy and uncharitableness. Let us have done with misunderstandings, let us strive to realize the dream of democracy by a prosperity of industry that shall mean the prosperity of the people, by a strengthening of our material resources that shall mean a strengthening of our character, by a merchandising that has for its end manhood, and womanhood, the ideal of American Citizenship.

XII

ON THE NATURE OF POLITICS

POLITICS is not an end, but a means. It is not a product, but a process. It is the art of government. Like other values it has its counterfeits. So much emphasis has been put upon the false that the significance of the true has been obscured and politics has come to convey the meaning of crafty and cunning selfishness, instead of candid and sincere service. The Greek derivation shows the nobler purpose. Politikos means city-rearing, state-craft. And when we remember that city also meant civilization, the spurious presentment, mean and sordid, drops away and the real figure of the politician, dignified and honorable, a minister to civilization, author and finisher of government, is revealed in its true and dignified proportions.

There is always something about genius

that is indefinable, mysterious, perhaps to
its possessor most of all. It has been the
product of rude surroundings no less than
of the most cultured environment, want
and neglect have sometimes nourished it,
abundance and care have failed to produce
it. Why some succeed in public life and
others fail would be as difficult to tell as
why some succeed or fail in other activities. Very few men in America have started
out with any fixed idea of entering public
life, fewer still would admit having such an
idea. It was said of Chief Justice Waite,
of the United States Supreme Court, being
asked when a youth what he proposed to
do when a man, he replied, he had not
yet decided whether to be President or
Chief Justice. This may be in part due to a
general profession of holding to the principle of Benjamin Franklin that office should
neither be sought nor refused and in part to
the American idea that the people choose
their own officers so that public service is

not optional. In other countries this is not so. For centuries some seats in the British Parliament were controlled and probably sold as were commissions in the army, but that has never been the case here. A certain Congressman, however, on arriving at Washington was asked by an old friend how he happened to be elected. He replied that he was not elected, but appointed. It is worth while noting that the boss who was then supposed to hold the power of appointment in that district has since been driven from power, but the Congressman, though he was defeated when his party was lately divided, has been reëlected. All of which suggests that the boss did not appoint in the first instance, but was merely well enough informed to see what the people wanted before they had formulated their own opinions and desires. It was said of McKinley that he could tell what Congress would do on a certain measure before the men in Congress themselves knew what their decision was to be. Cannon has said of McKinley that his ear was so close to the ground that it was full of grasshoppers. But the fact remains that office brokerage is here held in reprehensive scorn and professional office-seeking in contempt. Every native-born American, however, is potentially a President, and it must always be remembered that the obligation to serve the State is forever binding upon all, although office is the gift of the people.

Of course these considerations relate not to appointive places like the Judiciary, Commissionerships, clerical positions and like places, but to the more important elective offices. Another reason why political life of this nature is not chosen as a career is that it does not pay. Nearly all offices of this class are held at a financial sacrifice, not merely that the holder could earn more at some other occupation, but that the salary of the office does not maintain the holder of the office. It is but recently that

Parliament has paid a salary to its members. In years gone by the United States Senate has been rather marked for its number of rich men. Few prominent members of Congress are dependent on their salary, which is but another way of saying that in Washington Senators and Representatives need more than their official salaries to become most effective. It is a consolation to be able to state that this is not the condition of members of the Massachusetts General Court. There, ability and character come very near to being the sole requirements for success. Although some men have seen service in our legislature of nearly twenty years, to the great benefit of the Commonwealth, no one would choose that for a career and these men doubtless look on it only as an avocation.

For these reasons we have no profession of politics or of public life in the sense that we have a profession of law and medicine and other learned callings. We have men

who have spent many years in office, but **it**
would be difficult to find one outside the
limitations noted who would refer to that
as his business, occupation, or profession.

The inexperienced are prone to hold an
erroneous idea of public life and its methods.
Not long ago I listened to a joint debate in
a prominent preparatory school. Each side
took it for granted that public men were
influenced only by improper motives and
that officials of the government were seeking only their own gain and advantage without regard to the welfare of the people.
Such a presumption has no foundation in
fact. There are dishonest men in public
office. There are quacks, shysters, and
charlatans among doctors, lawyers, and
clergy, but they are not representative of
their professions nor indicative of their
methods. Our public men, as a class, are
inspired by honorable and patriotic motives,
desirous only of a faithful execution of their
trust from the executive and legislative

branches of the States and Nation down to the executives of our towns, who bear the dignified and significant title of selectmen. Public men must expect criticism and be prepared to endure false charges from their opponents. It is a matter of no great concern to them. But public confidence in government is a matter of great concern. It cannot be maintained in the face of such opinions as I have mentioned. It is necessary to differentiate between partisan assertions and actual conditions. It is necessary to recognize worth as well as to condemn graft. No system of government can stand that lacks public confidence and no progress can be made on the assumption of a false premise. Public administration is honest and sound and public business is transacted on a higher plane than private business.

There is no difficulty for men in college to understand elections and government. They have all had experience in it. The

same motives that operate in the choice
of class officers operate in choosing officers
for the Commonwealth. Here men are soon
estimated at their true worth. Here places
of trust are conferred and administered as
they will be in later years. The scale is
smaller, the opportunities are less, conditions are more artificial, but the principles
are the same. Of course the present esti-
mate is not the ultimate. There are men
here who appear important that will not
appear so in years to come. There are men
who seem insignificant now who will develop at a later day. But the motive which
leads to elections here leads to elections in
the State.

Is there any especial obligation on the
part of college-bred men to be candidates
for public office? I do not think so. It is
said that although college graduates constitute but one per cent of the population,
they hold about fifty per cent of the public
offices, so that this question seems to take

care of itself. But I do not feel that there is any more obligation to run for office than there is to become a banker, a merchant, a teacher, or enter any other special occupation. As indicated some men have a particular aptitude in this direction and some have none. Of course experience counts here as in any other human activity, and all experience worth the name is the result of application, of time and thought and study and practice. If the individual finds he has liking and capacity for this work, he will involuntarily find himself engaged in it. There is no catalogue of such capacity. One man gets results in one way, another in another. But in general only the man of broad sympathy and deep understanding of his fellow men can meet with much success.

What I have said relates to the somewhat narrow field of office-holding. This is really a small part of the American system or of any system. James Bryce tells us that we have a government of public opinion. That is growing to be more and more true of the governments of the entire world. The first care of despotism seems to be to control the school and the press. Where the mind is free it turns not to force but to reason for the source of authority. Men submit to a government of force as we are doing now when they believe it is necessary for their security, necessary to protect them from the imposition of force from without. This is probably the main motive of the German people. They have been taught that their only protection lay in the support of a military despotism. Rightly or wrongly they have believed this and believing have submitted to what they suppose their only means of security. They have been governed accordingly. Germany is still feudal.

This leads to the larger and all important field of politics. Here we soon see that office-holding is the incidental, but the standard of citizenship is the essential. Government does rest upon the opinions of men. Its results rest on their actions. This makes every man a politician whether he will or no. This lays the burden on us all. Men who have had the advantages of liberal culture ought to be the leaders in maintaining the standards of citizenship. Unless they can and do accomplish this result education is a failure. Greatly have they been taught, greatly must they teach. The power to think is the most practical thing in the world. It is not and cannot be cloistered from politics.

We live under a republican form of government. We need forever to remember that representative government does represent. A careless, indifferent representative is the result of a careless, indifferent electorate. The people who start to elect a man to get what he can for his district will probably find they have elected a man who will get what he can for himself. A body will keep on its course for a time after the moving impulse ceases by reason of its momentum. The men who founded our government had fought and thought mightily on the relationship of man to his government. Our institutions would go for a time under the momentum they gave. But we should be deluded if we supposed they can be maintained without more of the same stern sacrifice offered in perpetuity. Government is not an edifice that the founders turn over to posterity all completed. It is an institution, like a university which fails unless the process of education continues.

The State is not founded on selfishness. It cannot maintain itself by the offer of material rewards. It is the opportunity for service. There has of late been held out the hope that government could by legislation remove from the individual the need of effort. The managers of industries have seemed to think that their difficulties could be removed and prosperity ensured by changing the laws. The employee has been led to believe that his condition could be made easy by the same method. When industries can be carried on without any struggle, their results will be worthless, and when wages can be secured without any effort they will have no purchasing value. In the end the value of the product will be measured by the amount of effort necessary to secure it. Our late Dr. Garman recognized this limitation in one of his lecures where he says:—

"Critics have noticed three stages in the development of human civilization. First: the let-alone policy; every man to look out for number one. This is the age of selfishness. Second: the opposite pole of thinking; every man to do somebody's else work for him. This is the dry rot of sentimentality that feeds tramps and enacts poor laws such as excite the indignation of Herbert Spencer. But the third stage is represented by our formula: every man must render and receive the best possible service, except in the case of inequality, and there the strong must help the weak to help themselves; only on this condition is help given. This is the true interpretation of the life of Christ. On the first basis He would have remained in heaven and let the earth take care of itself. On the second basis He would have come to earth with his hands full of gold and silver treasures satisfying every want that unfortunate humanity could have devised. But on the third basis He comes to earth in the form of a servant who is at the same time a master commanding his disciples to take up their cross and follow Him; it is sovereignty through service as opposed to slavery through service. He refuses to make the world wealthy, but He offers to help them make themselves wealthy with true riches which shall be a hundred-fold more, even in this life, than that which was offered them by any former system."

This applies to political life no less than

to industrial life. We live under the fairest government on earth. But it is not self-sustaining. Nor is that all. There are selfishness and injustice and evil in the world. More than that, these forces are never at rest. Some desire to use the processes of government for their own ends. Some desire to destroy the authority of government altogether. Our institutions are predicated on the rights and the corresponding duties, on the worth, of the individual. It is to him that we must look for safety. We may need new charters, new constitutions and new laws at times. We must always have an alert and interested citizenship. We have no dependence but the individual. New charters cannot save us. They may appear to help but the chances are that the beneficial results obtained result from an increased interest aroused by discussing changes. Laws do not make reforms, reforms make laws. We cannot look to government. We must look to ourselves. We must stand not in the expectation of a reward but with a desire to serve. There will come out of government exactly what is put into it. Society gets about what it deserves. It is the part of educated men to know and recognize these principles and influences and knowing them to inform and warn their fellow countrymen. Politics is the process of action in public affairs. It is personal, it is individual, and nothing more. Destiny is in you.

XIII

TREMONT TEMPLE
November 3, 1917

There is a time and place for everything. There are times when some things are out of place. Domestic science is an important subject. So is the proper heating and ventilating of our habitations. But when the house is on fire reasonable men do not stop to argue of culinary cuts nor listen to a disquisition on plumbing; they call out the fire department and join it in an attempt to save their dwelling. They think only in terms of the conflagration.

So it is in this hour that has come to us so grim with destiny. We cannot stop now to discuss domestic party politics. Our men are on the firing-line of France. There will be no party designations in the casualty lists. We cannot stop to glance at that alluring field of history that tells us of the past patriotic devotion of the men of our party to the cause of the Nation — devotion without reserve. We must think now only in terms of winning the war.

An election at this time is not of our choosing. We are having one because it is necessary under the terms of our Constitution of Massachusetts. We have not conducted the ordinary party canvass. We have not flaunted party banners, we have not burned red fire, we have not rent the air with martial music, we have not held the usual party rallies. We have addressed meetings, but such addresses have been to urge subscriptions to the Liberty Loan, to urge gifts to the great humanitarian work of the Red Cross, and for the efforts of charity, benevolence, and mercy that are represented by the Y.M.C.A. and by the Knights of Columbus, for the conservation of food, and for the other patriotic purposes.

But we are not to infer that this is not an important election. It is too important to

think of candidates, too important to think
of party, too important to think of anything but our country at war. No more important election has been held since the
days of War Governor Andrew. On Tues-
day next the voters of Massachusetts will
decide whether they will support the Government in its defence of America, and its
defence of all that America means. There
is no room for domestic party issues here.
The only question for consideration is
whether the Government of this Commonwealth, legislative and executive, has rendered and will render prompt and efficient
support for the national defence. Perhaps
it would be enough to point out that Massachusetts troops were first at the Mexican
border and first in France. But that is only
part of the story.

Wars are waged now with far more than
merely the troops in the field. Every resource of the people goes into the battle. It
is a matter of organizing the entire fabric

of society. No one has yet pointed out, no one can point out, any failure on the part of our State Government to take efficient measures for this purpose. More than that, Massachusetts did not have to be asked; while Washington was yet dumb Massachusetts spoke.

Months before war was declared a Public Safety Committee was appointed and went to work; weeks before war a conference of New England Governors was called and a million dollars was given the Governor and Council to equip Massachusetts troops for which the National Treasury had no money. By reason of this foresight our men went forth better supplied than any others, with ten dollars additional pay from their home State, and the assurance that their dependents could draw forty dollars monthly where needed for their support. The production and distribution of food and fuel have been advanced. The maintenance of industrial peace has been promoted. The

Gloucester fishermen, fifteen thousand shoemakers in Lynn, the Boston & Maine railroad employees, have had their differences adjusted. A second million dollars for emergency expenses has been given the Governor and Council. An efficient State Guard of over ten thousand men has been organized. Our brave soldiers, their dependents, the great patriotic public have been protected by the present Government with every means that ingenuity could devise. We have won the right to reëlection by duty well performed.

Remember this: we are not responsible for the war, we are responsible for the preparation that enables us to defend our soldiers and ourselves from savages. Massachusetts is not going to repudiate these patriotic services. To do so now would mean more than repudiating the Government. It would mean repudiating the devotion of our brave men in arms, repudiating the sacrifice of the fathers, mothers, wives, and dear ones behind, and repudiating the loyalty of the millions who subscribed to the Liberty Loan,— it would mean repudiating America.

Massachusetts has decided that the path of the Mayflower shall not be closed. She has decided to sail the seas. She has decided to sail not under the edict of Potsdam, crimped in narrow lanes seeking safety in unarmed merchantmen painted in fantastic hues, as the badge of an infamous servitude, but she has decided to sail under the ancient Declaration of Independence, choosing what course she will, maintaining security by the guns of ships of the line, flying at the mast the Stars and Stripes, forever the emblem of a militant liberty.

XIV

DEDICATION OF TOWN-HOUSE, WESTON
NOVEMBER 27, 1917

I WAS interested to come out here and take part in the dedication of this beautiful building in part because my ancestors had lived in this locality in times gone past, but more especially because I am interested in the town governments of Massachusetts. You have heard the town-meeting referred to this evening. It seemed to me that the towns in this Commonwealth correspond in part to what we might call the water-tight compartments of the ship of state, and while sometimes our State Government has wavered, sometimes it has been suspended, and it has been thought that the people could not care for themselves under those conditions. Whenever that has arisen the towns of the Commonwealth have come to the rescue and been able to furnish the foundation and the strength on which might not only be carried on, but on which might again be erected the failing government of the Commonwealth or the failing government of the Nation. So that I know nothing to which we New Englanders owe more, and especially the people of Massachusetts, of our civil liberties than we do to our form of town government.

The history of Weston has been long and interesting, beginning, as your town seal designates, back in 1630, when Watertown was recognized as one of the three or four towns in the Commonwealth; set off by boundaries into the Farmers' Precinct in 1698, and becoming incorporated as a town in 1713. There begins a long and honorable history. Of course, the first part of it gathered to a large degree around the church. The first church was started here, I think, in 1695, and I believe that the land on which it was to be erected was purchased of a man who bore my name. Your first

clergyman seems to have been settled about
1702; and the long and even tenor of your
ways here and your devotion to things which
were established is perhaps shown and exemplified in the fact that during the next
one hundred and seventy-four years, coming clear down to 1876, you had but six
clergymen presiding over that church. You
have an example here now, along the same
line, in the long tenure of office that has
come to your present town clerk, he having been first elected, I believe, in 1864 and
having held office from that time to this,
probably serving as long, if not longer, than
any of the town clerks of Massachusetts,
certainly, I believe, the longest of any present living town clerk.

There are many interesting things connected with the history of this town. It
bore its part in the Indian Wars. Here was
organized an Indian fighting expedition
that went to the North, and, though some of
the men in that expedition were lost and the

expedition was not altogether successful, it showed the spirit, the resolution, the bravery, and the courage which animated the men of those days.

Mr. Young has referred to that day in Massachusetts history that we are all so proud of, the Nineteenth of April, 1775. But you had an interesting event here in this town leading up to that great day. General Gage was in command of the British forces at Boston. There had been gathered supplies for carrying on a war out here through Middlesex County and out to the west in Worcester. History tells us that he sent out here Sergeant Howe and other spies, in order that he might find out what the conditions were and whether it would be easy for the British troops to come out here and seize those supplies and break what they thought was the idea on the part of the colonists of starting a rebellion. Sergeant Howe came out here, went to the hotel, where, of course, the landlord received him hospitably, but informed him that probably it would n't be a healthy place for him to stay for a very long time, and sent him away in the dead of the night. He went back to Boston and made a report to the General in which he said that the people of this vicinity were generally resolved to be free or to die. That was the spirit of those times; and he advised the Britishers that if they wanted to go out to Worcester they would probably need an expedition of ten thousand men and a sufficient train of artillery, and he doubted whether, if such an expedition as that were sent out, any part of it would return alive. On account of the report that he brought back it was determined by the British authorities that it was more prudent to go up to Concord than it was to come out here on the way to Worcester. That was the reason that the expedition on that Nineteenth of April was started for Concord rather than through here for Worcester.

Of course, there are many other interesting events in the history of this town. You had here many men who have seen military service. You furnished a large number for the Revolutionary War and a large amount of money. You furnished as your quota one hundred and twenty-six soldiers that went into the army from 1861 to 1865. But you were doing here what they were doing all over the Commonwealth of Massachusetts. I doubt if the leading and prominent and decisive part that Massachusetts played in the great Revolutionary War is generally understood. It is interesting to recall that when General Washington came here he seems to have come with somewhat of a prejudice against New England men. I think there are extant letters which he wrote at that time rather reflecting upon what the New England men were doing and the character of Massachusetts men of those days. But that was not his idea at the end of the war. Then, although he had been brought

up far to the south, he had a different idea.
Then he said, and said very generously,
that he thought well of New England men
and had it not been for their support, had
it not been for the men, the materials and
munitions that they supplied to the Revolutionary forces, the war would not have
been a success. His name is interestingly
connected with your town of Weston.

You have had here not only an interesting population but an interesting location.
It was through this town that the great
arteries of travel ran to the west and south
and to the north. When Burgoyne surrendered, some of his troops were brought
through this town on their way to the sea-
coast. When Washington came up to visit
New England after he had been President,
he came through the town of Weston, and
I do not know whether this is any reflection on the cooking of those days in the
towns to the west, but it says in the history
of the town of Weston that at one time

when Washington stopped at the hotel in Wayland, although the hostess had provided what she thought was a very fine banquet, he left his staff to eat that and went out into the kitchen to help himself to a bowl of bread and milk. I suppose he would not be thought to have done that because he was a candidate for office and wanted to appear as one of the plain people, because that was after he had served in the office of President. But he stopped here in the town of Weston and was entertained here at the hotel. And many other great men passed through here and were entertained here from the time when we were colonies clear up to the time when the railroads were established along in the middle of the last century.

So this town has had a long and interesting history, and has done its part in building up Massachusetts and giving her strength to take her part in the history of this great Nation. And it is pleasant to see how the work that the fathers have done before us is bearing fruit in these times of ours. It is interesting to see this beautiful building. It is interesting to know that you have a town planning committee who are placing this building in a situation where it will contribute to the physical beauty of this historic town. We have not given the time and the attention and the thought that we should have given to things of that kind in Massachusetts. We have been too utilitarian. We have thought that if a building was located in some place where we could have access to it, where it could be used, where it could transact the business of the town, that was enough. We are coming to see in these modern days that that is not enough; that we need not only utilitarian motives, but that we need to give some time, some thought and attention to the artistic in life; that we need to concern ourselves not only with the material but give some thought to the spiritual; that we need to pay some attention to the beautiful as well as to that which is merely useful.

These things are appreciated. Weston is doing something along these lines and building her public buildings and laying out her public square or her common (as it was known in the old days) so they will be things of beauty as well as things of use. Let us dedicate this building to these new purposes. Let us dedicate it to the glorious history of the past. Let us dedicate it to the sacrifice that is required in these present days. Let us dedicate it to the hope of the future. Let us dedicate it to New England ideals — those ideals that have made Massachusetts one of the strong States of the Nation; strong enough so that in Revolutionary days we contributed far in excess of our portion of men and money to that great struggle; strong enough so that the whole Nation has looked to Massachusetts in days of stress for comfort and support.

We are very proud of our democracy. We are very proud of our form of government. We believe that there is no other nation on earth that gives to the individual the privileges and the rights that he has in America. The time has come now when we are going to defend those rights. The time has come when the world is looking to America, as the Nation has looked to Massachusetts in the past, to stand up and defend the rights of the individual. Sovereignty, it is our belief, is vested in the individual; and we are going to protect the rights of the individual. It is an auspicious moment to dedicate here in New England one of our town halls, an auspicious moment in which to dedicate it to the supremacy of those ideals for which the whole world is fighting at the present time; that the rights of the individual as they were established here in the past may be maintained by us now and carried to a yet greater development in the future.

XV

AMHERST ALUMNI DINNER
SPRINGFIELD
MARCH 15, 1918

THE individual may not require the higher institutions of learning, but society does. Without them civilization as we know it would fall from mankind in a night. They minister not alone to their own students, they minister to all humanity.

It is this same ancient spirit which, coming to the defence of the Nation, has in this new day of peril made nearly every college campus a training field for military service, and again sent graduate and undergraduate into the fighting forces of our country. They are demonstrating again that they are the strongholds of ordered liberty and individual freedom. This has ever been the distinguishing characteristic of the American institution of learning. They have believed in democracy because they believed in the nobility of man; they have served society because they have looked upon the possession of learning not as conferring a privilege but as laying on a duty. They have taught and practised the precept that the greater man's power the greater his obligation. The supreme choice is righteousness. It is that "moral power" to which Professor Tyler referred as the great contribution of college men to the cause of the Union.

The Nation is taking a military census, it is thinking now in terms of armament. The officers of government are discussing manpower, transportation by land and sea and through the air, the production of rifles, artillery, and explosives, the raising of money by loans and taxation. The Nation ought to be most mightily engaged in this work. It must put every ounce of its resources into the production and organization of its material power. But these are to a degree but the outward manifestations of something yet more important. The ultimate result of all wars and of this war has been and will be determined by the moral power of the nations engaged. On that will depend whether armies "ray out darkness" or are the source of light and life and liberty. Without the support of the moral power of the Nation armies will prove useless, without a moral victory, whatever the fortunes of the battlefield, there can be no abiding peace.

Whatever the difficulties of an exact definition may be the manifestations of moral power are not difficult to recognize. The life of America is rich with such examples. It has been predominant here. It established thirteen colonies which were to a large degree self-sustaining and self-governing. They fought and won a revolutionary war. What manner of men they were, what was the character of their leadership, was attested only in part by Saratoga and Yorktown. Washington had displayed great power on many fields of battle, the colonists had suffered long and endured to the end, but the glory of military power fades away beside the picture of the victorious general, returning his commission to the representatives of a people who would have made him king, and retiring after two terms from the Presidency which he could have held for life, and the picture of a war-worn people turning from debt, disorder, almost anarchy, not to division, not to despotism, but to national unity under the ordered liberty of the Federal Constitution.

It was manifested again in the adoption and defence by the young nation of that principle which is known as the Monroe Doctrine that European despotism should make no further progress in the Western Hemisphere. It is in the great argument of Webster replying to Hayne and the stout declaration of Jackson that he would treat nullification as treason. It was the compelling force of the Civil War, expounded by Lin-

coln in his unyielding purpose to save the
Union but "with malice toward none, with
charity for all," which General Grant, his
greatest soldier, put into practice at Appomattox when he sent General Lee back with
his sword, and his soldiers home to the
plantations, with their war horses for the
spring plowing. And at the conclusion of
the Spanish War it is to the ever-enduring
credit of our country that it exacted not
penalties, but justice, and actually compen-
sated a defeated foe for public property
that had come to our hands in the Philip-
pines as the result of the fortunes of battle.
But what of the present crisis? Is the heart
of the Nation still sound, does it still respond to the appeal to the high ideals of the
past? If those two and one half years, before the American declaration of war, shall
appear, when unprejudiced history is written, to have been characterized by patience,
forbearance, and self-restraint, they will
add to the credit of former days. If they

were characterized by selfishness, by politics, by a balancing of expediency against justice they will be counted as a time of ignominy for which a victorious war would furnish scant compensation.

XVI

MESSAGE FOR THE BOSTON POST
APRIL 22, 1918

THE nation with the greatest moral power will win. Of that are born armies and navies and the resolution to endure. Have faith in the moral power of America. It gave independence under Washington and freedom under Lincoln. Here, right never lost. Here, wrong never won. However powerful the forces of evil may appear, somewhere there are more powerful forces of righteousness. Courage and confidence are our heritage. Justice is our might. The outcome is in your hand, my fellow American; if you deserve to win, the Nation cannot lose.

XVII

ROXBURY HISTORICAL SOCIETY
BUNKER HILL DAY
JUNE 17, 1918

REVERENCE is the measure not of others but of ourselves. This assemblage on the one hundred and forty-third anniversary of the Battle of Bunker Hill tells not only of the spirit of that day but of the spirit of to-day. What men worship that will they become. The heroes and holidays of a people which fascinate their soul reveal what they hold are the realities of life and mark out a line beyond which they will not retreat, but at which they will stand to overcome or die. They who reverence Bunker Hill will fight there. Your true patriot sees home and hearthstone in the welfare of his country.

Rightly viewed, then, this day is set apart for an examination of ourselves by recounting the deeds of the men of long ago.

What was there in the events of the seven-teenth day of June, 1775, which holds the veneration of Americans and the increasing admiration of the world? There are the physical facts not too unimportant to be unworthy of reiteration even in the learned presence of an Historical Society. A de-tachment of men clad for the most part in the dress of their daily occupations, stand-ing with bared heads and muskets grounded muzzle down in the twilight glow on Cam-bridge Common, heard Samuel Langdon, President of Harvard College, seek divine blessing on their cause and marched away in the darkness to a little eminence at Charlestown, where, ere the setting of an-other sun, much history was to be made and much glory lost and won. When a new dawn had lifted the mists of the Bay, the British, under General Howe, saw an in-trenchment on Breed's Hill, which must be taken or Boston abandoned. The works were exposed in the rear to attack from land and sea. This was disdained by the king's soldiers in their contempt for the supposed fighting ability of the Americans. Leisurely, as on dress parade, they assembled for an assault that they thought was to be a demonstration of the uselessness of any armed resistance on the part of the Colonies. In splendid array they advanced late in the day. A few straggling shots and all was still behind the parapet. It was easier than they had expected. But when they reached a point where 't is said the men behind the intrenchments could see the whites of their eyes, they were met by a withering fire that tore their ranks asunder and sent them back in disorder, utterly routed by their despised foes. In time they form and advance again but the result is the same. The demonstration of superiority was not a success. For a third time they form, not now for dress parade, but for a hazardous assault. This time the result was different. The patriots had lost nothing of courage or determination but there was left scarcely one round of powder. They had no bayonets. Pouring in their last volley and still resisting with clubbed muskets, they retired slowly and in order from the field. So great was the British loss that there was no pursuit. The intensity of the battle is told by the loss of the Americans, out of about fifteen hundred engaged, of nearly twenty per cent, and of the British, out of some thirty-five hundred engaged, of nearly thirty-three per cent, all in one and one half hours.

It was the story of brave men bravely led but insufficiently equipped. Their leader, Colonel Prescott, had walked the breastworks to show his men that the cannonade was not particularly dangerous. John Stark, bringing his company, in which were his Irish compatriots, across Charlestown Neck under the guns of the battleships, refused to quicken his step. His Major, Andrew McCleary, fell at the rail fence which he had

held during the day. Dr. Joseph Warren,
your own son of Roxbury, fell in the retreat, but the Americans, though picking
off his officers, spared General Howe. They
had fought the French under his brother.

Such were some of the outstanding deeds
of the day. But these were the deeds of men
and the deeds of men always have an in-
ward significance. In distant Philadelphia,
on this very day, the Continental Congress
had chosen as the Commander of their
Army, General George Washington, a man
whose clear vision looked into the realities
of things and did not falter. On his way
to the front four days later, dispatches
reached him of the battle. He revealed the
meaning of the day with one question,
"Did the militia fight?" Learning how
those heroic men fought, he said, "Then
the liberties of the Country are safe." No
greater commentary has ever been made on
the significance of Bunker Hill.

We read events by what goes before and

after. We think of Bunker Hill as the first
real battle for independence, the prelude to
the Revolution. Yet these were both after-
thoughts. Independence Day was still more
than a year away and then eight years from
accomplishment. The Revolution cannot be
said to have become established until the
adoption of the Federal Constitution. No,
on this June day, these were not the con-
scious objects sought. They were contending for the liberties of the country, they
were not yet bent on establishing a new nation nor on recognizing that relationship
between men which the modern world calls
democracy. They were maintaining well
their traditions, these sons of Londonderry,
lovers of freedom and anxious for the fray,
and these sons of the Puritans, whom Macaulay tells us humbly abased themselves in
the dust before the Lord, but hesitated not
to set their foot upon the neck of their
king.

It is the moral quality of the day that

abides. It was the purpose of those plain garbed men behind the parapet that told whether they were savages bent on plunder, living under the law of the jungle, or sons of the morning bearing the light of civilization. The glorious revolution of 1688 was fading from memory. The English Government of that day rested upon privilege and corruption at the base, surmounted by a king bent on despotism, but fortunately too weak to accomplish any design either of good or ill. An empire still outwardly sound was rotting at the core. The privilege which had found Great Britain so complacent sought to establish itself over the Colonies. The purpose of the patriots was resistance to tyranny. Pitt and Burke and Lord Camden in England recognized this, and, loving liberty, approved the course of the Colonies. The Tories here, loving privilege, approved the course of the Royal Government. Bunker Hill meant that the Colonies would save themselves and saving them-

selves save the mother country for liberty.
The war was not inevitable. Perhaps wars
are never inevitable. But the conflict between freedom and privilege was inevitable.
That it broke out in America rather than
in England was accidental. Liberty, the
rights of man against tyranny, the rights
of kings, was in the air. One side must give
way. There might have been a peaceful
settlement by timely concessions such as
the Reform Bill of England some fifty
years later, or the Japanese reforms of our
own times, but wanting that a collision was
inevitable. Lacking a Bunker Hill there had
been another Dunbar.

The eighteenth century was the era of
the development of political rights. It was
the culmination of the ideas of the Renaissance. It was the putting into practice in
government of the answer to the long pondered and much discussed question, "What
is right?" Custom was giving way at last
to reason. Class and caste and place, all the

distinctions based on appearance and accident were giving way before reality. Men turned from distinctions which were temporal to those which were eternal. The sovereignty of kings and the nobility of peers was swallowed up in the sovereignty and nobility of all men. The inequal in quantity became equal in quality.

The successful solution of this problem was the crowning glory of a century and a half of America. It established for all time how men ought to act toward each other in the governmental relation. The rule of the people had begun.

Bunker Hill had a deeper significance. It was an example of the great law of human progress and civilization. There has been much talk in recent years of the survival of the fittest and of efficiency. We are beginning to hear of the development of the super-man and the claim that he has of right dominion over the rest of his inferiors on earth. This philosophy denies the doc-

trine of equality and holds that government
is not based on consent but on compulsion.
It holds that the weak must serve the strong,
which is the law of slavery, it applies the
law of the animal world to mankind and
puts science above morals. This sounds the
call to the jungle. It is not an advance to
the morning but a retreat to night. It is not
the light of human reason but the darkness
of the wisdom of the serpent.

The law of progress and civilization is
not the law of the jungle. It is not an earthly
law, it is a divine law. It does not mean the
survival of the fittest, it means the sacrifice of the fittest. Any mother will give her
life for her child. Men put the women and
children in the lifeboats before they themselves will leave the sinking ship. John
Hampden and Nathan Hale did not survive, nor did Lincoln, but Benedict Arnold
did. The example above all others takes us
back to Jerusalem some nineteen hundred
years ago. The men of Bunker Hill were

true disciples of civilization, because they were willing to sacrifice themselves to resist the evils and redeem the liberties of the British Empire. The proud shaft which rises over their battlefield and the bronze form of Joseph Warren in your square are not monuments to expediency or success, they are monuments to righteousness.

This is the age-old story. Men are reading it again to-day — written in blood. The Prussian military despotism has abandoned the law of civilization for the law of barbarism. We could approve and join in the scramble to the jungle, or we could resist and sacrifice ourselves to save an erring nation. Not being beasts, but men, we choose the sacrifice.

This brings us to the part that America is taking at the end of its second hundred and fifty years of existence. Is it not a part of that increasing purpose which the poet, the seer, tells us runs through the ages? Has not our Nation been raised up and strengthened, trained and prepared, to meet the great sacrifice that must be made now to save the world from despotism? We have heard much of our lack of preparation. We have been altogether lacking in preparation in a strict military sense. We had no vast forces of artillery or infantry, no large stores of munitions, few trained men. But let us not forget to pay proper respect to the preparation we did have, which was the result of long training and careful teaching. We had a mental, a moral, a spiritual training that fitted us equally with any other people to engage in this great contest which after all is a contest of ideas as well as of arms. We must never neglect the military preparation again, but we may as well recognize that we have had a preparation without which arms in our hands would very much resemble in purpose those now arrayed against us.

Are we not realizing a noble destiny? The great Admiral who discovered America bore the significant name of Christopher. It has been pointed out that this name means Christ-bearer. Were not the men who stood at Bunker Hill bearing light to the world by their sacrifices? Are not the men of to-day, the entire Nation of to-day, living in accordance with the significance of that name, and by their service and sacrifice redeeming mankind from the forces that make for everlasting destruction? We seek no territory and no rewards. We give but do not take. We seek for a victory of our ideas. Our arms are but the means. America follows no such delusion as a place in the sun for the strong by the destruction of the weak. America seeks rather, by giving of her strength for the service of the weak, a place in eternity.

XVIII
FAIRHAVEN
JULY 4, 1918

WE have met on this anniversary of American independence to assess the dimensions of a kind deed. Nearly four score years ago the master of a whaling vessel sailing from this port rescued from a barren rock in the China Sea some Japanese fishermen. Among them was a young boy whom he brought home with him to Fairhaven, where he was given the advantages of New England life and sent to school with the boys and girls of the neighborhood, where he excelled in his studies. But as he grew up he was filled with a longing to see Japan and his aged mother. He knew that the duty of filial piety lay upon him according to the teachings of his race, and he was determined to meet that obligation. I think that is one of the lessons of this day. Here was a youth who determined to pursue the course which he had been taught was right. He braved the dangers of the voyage and the greater dangers that awaited an absentee from his country under the then existing laws, to perform his duty to his mother and to his native land. In making that return I think we are entitled to say that he was the first Ambassador of America to the Court of Japan, for his extraordinary experience soon brought him into the association of the highest officials of his country, and his presence there prepared the way for the friendly reception which was given to Commodore Perry when he was sent to Japan to open relations between that Government and the Government of America.

And so we see how out of the kind deed of Captain Whitefield, friendly relations which have existed for many years between the people of Japan and the people of America were encouraged and made possible. And it is in recognition of that event that we have here to-day this great concourse of people, this martial array, and the representative of the Japanese people — a people who have never failed to respond to an act of kindness.

It was with special pleasure that I came here representing the Commonwealth of Massachusetts, to extend an official welcome to His Excellency Viscount Ishii, who comes here to present to the town of Fairhaven a Sumari sword on behalf of the son of that boy who was rescued long ago. This sword was once the emblem of place and caste and arbitrary rank. It has taken on a new significance because Captain Whitefield was true to the call of humanity, because a Japanese boy was true to his call of duty. This emblem will hereafter be a token not only of the friendship that exists between two nations but a token of liberty, of freedom, and of the recognition by the Government of both these nations of the rights of the people. Let it remain here as a mutual pledge by the giver and the receiver of their determination that the motive which inspired the representatives of each race to do right is to be a motive which is to govern the people of the earth.

XIX

SOMERVILLE REPUBLICAN CITY COMMITTEE
AUGUST 7, 1918

COMING into your presence in ordinary times, gentlemen of the committee, I should be inclined to direct your attention to the long and patriotic services of our party, to the great benefits its policies have conferred upon this Nation, to the illustrious names of our leaders, to our present activities, and to our future party policy. But these are not ordinary times. Our country is at war. There is no way to save our party if our country be lost. And in the present crisis there is only one way to save our country. We must support the State and National Governments in whatever they request for the conduct of the war. The Constitution makes the President Commander-in-Chief of the Army and Navy. What he needs should be freely given. This has been and will be the policy of the Republican administration of Massachusetts and of her Senators and Representatives in Congress. We seek no party advantage from the distress of our country. Among Republicans there will be no political profiteering.

It is a year and four months now since we declared the German Government was making war on America. We are beginning to see what our requirements are. We had a small but efficient standing army, and a larger but less efficient National Guard. These have been increased by enlistments. We have a new national force, — never to be designated as Conscripts, but as the accepted soldiers of a whole Nation that has volunteered, of almost unlimited numbers. By taxation and by three Liberty Loans, each over-subscribed by more than fifty per cent, we have demonstrated that there will be no lack of money. The problem of the production and conservation of food is being met, though not yet without some inconvenience, yet so far with very little suffering. The remaining factor is the production of the necessary materials for carrying on the war. We lack ships and military supplies. Whether these are secured in time in sufficient quantity will depend in a large measure upon the attitude of the people managing and employed in these industries. The attitude of the leaders of organized labor has been patriotic. They realize that this is a war to preserve the rights that have been won for the people, and they have at all times advised their fellow workmen to remain at work. There must be forbearance on all sides. Where wages are too low they should be increased voluntarily. Where there is disagreement the Government has provided means for investigation and adjustment. Our industrial front must keep pace with our military front.

We are demonstrating the ability of America. Within the last few days the report has come to us that our soldiers have defeated the Prussian Guard. The sneer of Germany at America is vanishing. It is true that the German high command still couple American and African soldiers together in intended derision. What they say in scorn, let us say in praise. We have fought before for the rights of all men irrespective of color. We are proud to fight now with colored men for the rights of white men. It would be fitting recognition of their worth to send our American negro, when that time comes, to inform the Prussian military despotism on what terms their defeated armies are to be granted peace.

While the victories that have recently come to our arms are most encouraging, they should only stimulate us to redoubled efforts. The only hope of a short war is to prepare for a long one. In this work the States play a most important part. Massachusetts must be kept so organized and governed as to continue that able, effective, and prompt coöperation with the National Government that has marked the past progress of the war. In this we have a great part to do here. It was for such a task that the Republican Party came into being sixty-four years ago. One of the resolutions adopted at its birth peculiarly dedicates it to the requirements of the present hour.

"Resolved, that in view of the necessity of battling for the first principles of republican government and against the schemes of an aristocracy, the most revolting and oppressive with which the earth was ever cursed, or man debased, we will coöperate and be known as 'Republicans' until the contest be terminated."

This great work lies before our party in Massachusetts. We shall go on battling for the first principles of Republican government until it has been secured to all the people of the earth.

Our American forces on sea and land are proving sufficient to turn the tide in favor of the Allied cause. They could not succeed alone, we could not succeed alone. We are furnishing a reserve power that is bringing victory.

But America must furnish more than armies and navies for the future. If armies and navies were to be supreme, Germany would be right. There are other and greater forces in the world than march to the roll of the drum. As we are turning the scale with our sword now, so hereafter we must turn the scale with the moral power of America. It must be our disinterested plans that are to restore Europe to a place through justice when we have secured victory through the sword. And into a new world we are to take not only the people of oppressed Europe but the people of America. Out of our sacrifice and suffering, out of our blood and tears, America shall have a new awakening, a rededication to the cause of Washington and Lincoln, a firmer conviction for the right.

XX

WRITTEN FOR THE SUNDAY ADVERTISER AND AMERICAN

September 1, 1918

The man who seeks to stimulate and increase the production of materials necessary for the conduct of the war by raising the price he pays is a patriot. The man who refuses to sell at a fine price whatever he may have that is necessary for the conduct of the war is a profiteer. One man seeks to help his country at his own expense, the other seeks to help himself at his country's expense. One is willing to suffer himself that his country may prosper, the other is willing his country should suffer that he may prosper.

In ordinary times these difficulties are taken care of by the operation of the law of supply and demand. If the price is too high the buyer has time to go elsewhere. In war the element of time is one of the chief considerations. When what is wanted is once found it must be made available at once. The principle of trusteeship also comes into more immediate operation. It is recognized in time of peace that the public may take what it may need of private property for the general welfare, paying a fair compensation, and that the right to own property carries with it the duty of using it for the welfare of our fellow man. The time has gone by when one may do what he will with his own. He must use his property for the general good or the very right to hold private property is lost.

These are some of the rules to be observed in the relationship between man and man. To see that these rules are properly enforced, governments are formed. When they are not observed — when the strong refuse voluntary justice to the weak — then it is time for the strong arm of the law through the public officers to intervene and see that the weak are protected. This can usually be done by the enactment of a law which all will try to obey, but when this course has failed there is no remedy save by the process of law to take from the wrong-doer his power in the future to do harm.

America is built on faith in the individual, faith in his will and power to do right of his own accord, but equally is the determination that the individual shall be protected against whatsoever force may be brought against him. We believe in him not because of what he has, but what he is. But this is a practical faith. It does not rest on any silly assumption that virtue is the reward of anything but effort or that liberty can be secured at the price of anything but eternal vigilance.

It is in recognition of these principles and conditions that the General Court of last year gave the Governor power to make rules for the use by individuals of their property during the war for the general defence of the Commonwealth, and on failure on their part so to use their property, to take possession of it for such term as may be necessary. Up to the present time it has not been necessary to take property. Our faith in the patriotism of our citizens has been amply demonstrated. Of our four millions of people few have failed voluntarily to use their every resource for the defence of the Nation. But of late there have been some complaints of too high charges for rent in war-material centres. In some cases patriotic workmen engaged in labor most vital to our country's salvation have been threatened with eviction by profiteering landlords unless they paid exorbitant rents. No one is undertaking to say that rents must on no account be raised. But the Executive Department of Massachusetts is undertaking to say that in any case where rents are unreasonably raised to the detriment of people who are just as essential to our victory as the soldier in the field, if any one is to be evicted from such premises it will be the persons who are raising rents and not the persons who are asked to pay them. This action is taken to protect the Nation. It is taken in our desire and determination here to coöperate with the Federal Government in every activity that is necessary to the prosecution of the war. It is taken also for the protection of the individual. We do not care how humble he may be, we do not care how exalted the landlord may be, justice shall be done.

This is not to be taken as an offer on the part of the Commonwealth to have unloaded on it a large amount of property at a high price. Possession may be taken, but the ownership will not change. Unless reasonable rents are charged, the tenant will stay in possession, but the rent which the Commonwealth shall pay for occupation will be determined by a jury. This means justice, nothing more, nothing less — justice to the tenant, justice to the landlord. It is not to be inferred that our real estate owners have lacked anything as a class in patriotism. They are our most loyal, most self-sacrificing, most commendable citizens. Massachusetts by its Homestead Commission is encouraging its citizens to own real estate because such ownership is a sheet anchor to self-government. But it is a proclamation of warning to profiteers, of approbation and approval to patriots, and of assurance and assistance to the working people and rent payers of our Commonwealth.

XXI

ESSEX COUNTY CLUB, LYNNFIELD
September 14, 1918

WE meet here to-day as the inheritors of those principles which preserved our Nation and extended its constitutional guaranties to all its citizens. We come not as partisans but as patriots. We come to pledge anew our faith in all that America means and to declare our firm determination to defend her within and without from every foe. Above that we come to pay our tribute of wonder and admiration at the great achievements of our Nation and at the glory which they are shedding around her.

The past four years has shown the world the existence of a conspiracy against mankind of a vastness and a wickedness that could only be believed when seen in operation and confessed by its participants. This conspiracy was promoted by the German military despotism. It probably was encouraged by the results of three wars — one against Denmark which robbed her of territory, one against Austria which robbed her of territory, and one against France which robbed her of territory and a cash indemnity of a billion dollars. These seemingly easy successes encouraged their perpetrators to plan for the pillage and enslavement of the earth.

To accomplish this, the German despotism began at home. By a systematic training the whole German people were perverted. A false idea of their own greatness was added to their contempt and hate of other nations, who, they were taught, were bent on their destruction. The military class were exalted and all else degraded. Thus was laid the foundation for the atrocities which have marked their conduct of the war.

The vastness of the conquest planned has recently been revealed by August Thyssen, one of the greatest steel men of the empire. He tells of a calling together, in the years before the war, of the industrial and banking interests of the Nation, when a plan of war was laid before them, and their support secured by the promise of spoils. France, India, Canada, Australia were to be given over to German satraps. His share was 30,000 acres in Australia, with $750,- 000 provided by the Government for its development. This was the promise made by the Kaiser. Here was the motive of the war.

How it was provoked is told by Prince Lichnowski, the Ambassador of Germany to London. He shows how he had reached agreements for a treaty which would show the good will of Great Britain. Berlin refused to sign it unless it should be kept secret. He shows how Germany used Austria to attack Serbia; how mediations were refused; when Austria was about to withdraw, Germany sent an ultimatum to Russia one day and the next day declared war.

This diplomat sums up the whole case when he says: "I had to support in London a policy the heresy of which I recognized. That brought down vengeance on me because it was a sin against the Holy Ghost." What an indictment of Germany from her own confession! A plan to use the revelations of science for the sack and slavery of the earth; the degradation, perversion, corruption of a whole people, and by those who should have been the wardens of their righteousness, done for the temporal glory of a military caste, and all in the name of divine right.

Much of this was not known in America when we declared war. It is with great difficulty we realize it now. We had seen Germany going from infamy to infamy. We did know of the violated treaty of Belgium, of the piracy, the murder of women and children, the destruction of the property and lives of our neutral citizens, and finally the plain declaration of the German Im-

perial Government that it would wantonly
and purposely destroy the property and
lives of any American citizen who exercised
his undoubted legal right to sail certain portions of the sea. This attempt to declare
law for America by an edict from Potsdam
we resisted by the sword. We see at last not
only the hideous wickedness which perpe-
trated the war, we see that it is a world war,
that Germany struck not only at Belgium,
she struck at us, she struck at our whole
system of civilization. A wicked purpose,
which a vain attempt to realize has involved
its authors in more and more wickedness.
We hear that even among the civil population of Germany crime is rampant.

Looking now at this condition of Germany and her Allies, it is time to inquire
what America and her Allies have to offer
as a remedy, and what effect the application
of such remedy has had upon ourselves. We
have drawn the sword, but is it only to

"Be blood for blood, for treason treachery?"

Are we seeking merely to match infamy with infamy, merely to pillage and destroy those who threatened to pillage and destroy us? No; we have taken more than the sword, lest we perish by the sword; we have summoned the moral power of the Nation. We have recognized that evil is only to be overcome by good. We have marshalled the righteousness of America to overwhelm the wickedness of Germany. A new spirit has come over the nation the like of which was never seen before. We can see it not only in the new purity of camp life, in the heroism of our soldiers as they fight in the faith and for the faith of the fathers, but we see it in the healing influences which a righteous purpose has had upon the evils which beset us.

We entered the war a people of many nationalities. We are united now; every one is first an American. We were beset with jealousies, and envy, and class prejudice. Service in the camp has taught each soldier to respect the other, whatever his source, and a mutual sympathy at home has brought all into a common citizenship. The service flag is a great leveller.

Our industrial life has been purified of prejudice. No one is complaining now that any concern is too large, too strong. All see that the great organizations of capital in industry are our salvation. Labor has taken on a new dignity and nobility. When the idle see the necessity of work, when we begin to recognize industry as essential, the working man begins to have paid him the honor which is his due.

Invention, chemistry, medicine, surgery, have been stimulated and improved. Even our agriculture has taken on more economical methods and increased production.

The call for man power has given a new idea of the importance of the individual, so that there has been brought to the humblest the knowledge that he was not only important but his importance was realized.

And with this has come the discovery of new powers, not only in the slouch whom military drill has transformed into a man, but to labor that has found a new joy, satisfaction and efficiency in its work. The entire activities of the Nation are tuned up.

The spirit of charity has been aroused. Hundreds of millions have been provided by voluntary gifts for the Red Cross, Knights of Columbus, Hebrew Charities, and Christian Associations. The people are turning to their places of worship with a new religious fervor. Everywhere selfishness is giving way to service, idleness to industry, wastefulness to thrift.

The war is being won. It is being overwhelmingly won. A righteous purpose has not only strengthened our arms abroad but exalted the Nation at home.

The great work before us is to keep this new spirit in the right path. The opportunity for a military training, the beneficial results of its discipline, must be continued for the youth of our country. The sacrifice necessary for national defence must hereafter never be neglected. The virtues of war must be carried into peace. But this must not be done at the expense of the freedom of the individual. It must be the expression of self-government and not the despotism of a German military caste or a Russian Bolshevik state. We are in this war to preserve the institutions that have made us great. The war has revealed to us their true greatness. All argument about the efficiency of despotism and the incompetence of republics was answered at the Marne and will be hereafter answered at the Rhine. We are not going to overcome the Kaiser by becoming like him, nor aid Russia by becoming like her.

We see now that Prussian despotism was the natural ally of the Russian Bolshevik and the I.W.W. here. Both exist to pervert and enslave the people; both seek to break down the national spirit of the world

for their own wicked ends. Both are doomed
to failure. By taking our place in the world,
America is to become more American, as
by doing his duty the individual develops
his own manhood. We see now that when
the individual fails, whether it be from a
despotism or the dead level of a socialistic
state, all has failed.

A new vision has come to the Nation, a
vision that must never be obscured. It is
for us to heed it, to follow it. It is a revelation, but a revelation not of our weakness
but of our strength, not of new principles,
but of the power that lies in the application
of old doctrines. May that vision never
fade, may America inspired by a great purpose ever be able to say,

"Mine eyes have seen the glory of the coming of
the Lord."

XXII

TREMONT TEMPLE
November 2, 1918

To the greatest task man ever undertook
our Commonwealth has applied itself, will
continue to apply itself with no laggard
hand. One hundred and ninety thousand
of her sons already in the field, hundreds of
millions of her treasure contributed to the
cause, her entire citizenship moved with a
single purpose, all these show a determination unalterable, to prosecute the war to a
victory so conclusive, to a destruction of all
enemy forces so decisive, that those im-
pious pretentions which have threatened
the earth for many years will never be renewed. There can be no discussion about it,
there can be no negotiation about it. The
country is united in the conviction that the
only terms are unconditional surrender.

This determination has arisen from no

sudden impulse or selfish motive. It was forced upon us by the plan and policy of Germany and her methods of waging war upon others. The main features of it all have long been revealed while each day brings to light more of the details. We have seen the studied effort to make perverts of sixty millions of German people. We know of the corrupting of the business interests of the Empire to secure their support. We know that war had been decreed before the pretext on which it was declared had happened. We know Austria was and is the creature of Germany. We have beheld the violation of innocent Belgium, the hideous outrages on soldier and civilian, the piracy, the murder of our own neutral citizens, and finally there came the notice, which as an insult to America has been exceeded only by the recent suggestion that we negotiate a peace with its authors, — the notice claiming dominion over our citizens and authority to exclude our ships from the sea. The great

pretender to the throne of the earth thought
the time had come to assert that we were
his subjects. Two millions of our men already in France, and each day ten thousand more are hastening to pay their respects to him at his court in Berlin in person. He has our answer.

It would be a mistake to suppose we have
already won the war. It is not won yet, but
we have reached the place where we know
how to win it, and if we continue our ex-
ertions we shall win it fully, completely,
grandly, as becomes a great people contending for the cause of righteousness.

We entered the war late and without
previous military preparation. The more
clearly we discern the beginning and the
progress of the struggle, the more we must
admire the great spirit of those nations by
whose side we fight. The more we know of
the terrible price they paid, the matchless
sacrifices they magnificently endured — the
French, the Italians, the British, the Bel-

gians, the Serbians, the Poles, and the mis-governed, misguided people of Russia — the bravery of their soldiers in the field, the unflinching devotion of their people at home, and remember that in no small sense they were doing this for us, that we have been the direct beneficiaries of peoples who have given their all, the less disposition we have to think too much of our own importance. But all this should not cause us to withhold the praise that is due our own Army and Navy, or to overlook the fact that our people have met every call that patriotism has made. The soldiers and sailors who fight under the Stars and Stripes are the most magnificent body of men that ever took up arms for defence of a great cause. Man for man they surpass any other troops on earth.

We must not forget these things. We must not neglect to record them for the information of generations to come. The names and records of boards and commissions, relief societies, of all who have engaged in financing the cause of government and charity, and other patriotic work, should be preserved in the Library of the Commonwealth, and with these, our military achievements. These will show how American soldiers met and defeated the Prussian Guard. They will show also that in all the war no single accomplishment, on a like scale, excelled the battle of St. Mihiel, carried out by American troops, with our own Massachusetts boys among them, and that the first regiment to be decorated as a regiment for conspicuous service and gallantry in our Army in France was the 104th, formerly of the old Massachusetts National Guard. Such is our record and it cannot be forgotten.

In reaching the great decision to enter the war, in preparing the answer which speaks with so much authority, in the only language that despotism can understand, America has arisen to a new life. We have taken a new place among the nations. The Revolution made us a nation; the Spanish War made us a world power, the present war has given us recognition as a world power. We shall not again be considered provincial. Whether we desired it or not this position has come to us with its duties and its responsibilities.

This new position should not be misunderstood. It does not mean any diminution of our national spirit. It rather means that it should be intensified. The most outstanding feature of the war has been the assertion of the national spirit. Each nationality is contending for the right to have its own government, and in that is meeting with the sanction of the free peoples of the earth. We are discussing a league of nations. Such a league, if formed, is not for the purpose, must not be for the purpose, of diminishing the spirit or influence of our Nation, but to make that spirit and influence more real and more effective. Believing in our Nation thoroughly and unreservedly, confident that the evidence of the past and present justifies that belief, it is our one desire to make America more American. There is no greater service that we can render the oppressed of the earth than to maintain inviolate the freedom of our own citizens.

Under our National Government the States are the sheet-anchors of our institutions. On them falls the task of administering local affairs and of supporting the National, Government in peace and war. The success with which Massachusetts has met her local problems, the efficiency with which she has placed her resources of men and materials at the disposal of the Nation, has been unsurpassed. The efficient organization of the Commonwealth, which has proved itself in time of stress, must be maintained undiminished. On the States will largely fall the task of putting into effect the lessons of the war that are to make America more truly American.

One of our first duties is military training. The opportunity hereafter for the youth of the Nation to receive instruction in the science of national defence should be universal. The great problem which our present experience has brought is the development of man power. This includes many questions, but especially public health and mental equipment. Sanitation and education will require more attention in the future.

America has been performing a great service for humanity. In that service we have arisen to a new glory. The people of the nation without distinction have been performing a great service for America. In it they have realized a new citizenship. Prussianism fails. Americanism succeeds. Education is to teach men not what to think but how to think. Government will take on new activities, but it is not more to control the people, the people are more to control the Government.

We have come to the realization of a new brotherhood among nations and among men. It came through the performance of a common duty. A brotherhood that existed unseen has been recognized at last by those called to the camp and trenches and those working for their victory at home. This spirit must not be misunderstood. It is not a gospel of ease but of work, not of dependence but of independence, not of an easy tolerance of wrong but a stern insistence on right, not the privilege of receiving but the duty of giving.

"Man proposes but God disposes." When Germany lit up her long toasted day with the lurid glare of war, she thought the end of freedom for the peoples of the earth had come. She thought that the power of her sword was hereafter to reign supreme over a world in slavery, and that the divine right of a king was to be established forever. We have seen the drama drawing to its close. It has shown the victory of justice and of freedom and established the divine rights of the people. Through it is shining a new revelation of the true brotherhood of man. As we see the purpose Germany sought and the result she will secure, the words of Holy Writ come back to us — "The wrath of man shall praise Him."

XXIII

FANEUIL HALL
NOVEMBER 4, 1918

WE need a word of caution and of warning. I am responsible for what I have said and what I have done. I am not responsible for what my opponents say I have said or say I have done either on the stump or in untrue political advertisements and untrue posters. I shall not deal with these. I do not care to touch them, but I do not want any of my fellow citizens to misunderstand my ignoring them as expressing any attitude other than considering such attempts unworthy of notice when men are fighting for the preservation of our country.

Our work is drawing to a close — our patriotic efforts. We have had in view but one object — the saving of America.

We shall accomplish that object first by winning the war. That means a great deal. It means getting the world forever rid of the German idea. We can see no way to do this but by a complete surrender by Germany to the Allies.

We stand by the State and National Governments in the prosecution of this object. I have reiterated that we support the Commander-in-Chief in war work. He says that is so.

We want no delay in prosecuting the war. The quickest way is the way to save most lives and treasure. We want to care for the soldiers and their dependents. That has been the recognized duty of the Government for generations.

To save America means to save American institutions, it means to save the manhood and womanhood of our country. To that we are pledged.

There will be great questions of reconstruction, social, industrial, economic and governmental questions, that must be met and solved. They must be met with a recognition of a new spirit.

It is a time to keep our faith in our State, our Nation, our institutions, and in each other. Doing that, the war will be won in the field and won in civil life at home.

XXIV

FROM INAUGURAL ADDRESS AS GOVERNOR
JANUARY 2, 1919

You are coming to a new legislative session under the inspiration of the greatest achievements in all history. You are beholding the fulfilment of the age-old promise, man coming into his own. You are to have the opportunity and responsibility of reflecting this new spirit in the laws of the most enlightened of Commonwealths. We must steadily advance. Each individual must have the rewards and opportunities worthy of the character of our citizenship, a broader recognition of his worth and a larger liberty, protected by order — and always under the law. In the promotion of human welfare Massachusetts happily may not need much reconstruction, but, like all living organizations, forever needs continuing construction. What are the lessons of the past? How shall they be applied to these days of readjustment? How shall we emerge from the autocratic methods of war to the democratic methods of peace, raising ourselves again to the source of all our strength and all our glory — sound self-government?

It is your duty not only to reflect public opinion, but to lead it. Whether we are to enter a new era in Massachusetts depends upon you. The lessons of the war are plain. Can we carry them on into peace? Can we still act on the principle that there is no sacrifice too great to maintain the right? Shall we continue to advocate and practise thrift and industry? Shall we require unswerving loyalty to our country? These are the foundations of all greatness.

Let there be a purpose in all your legislation to recognize the right of man to be well born, well nurtured, well educated, well employed, and well paid. This is no gospel of ease and selfishness, or class distinction, but a gospel of effort and service, of universal application.

Such results cannot be secured at once, but they should be ever before us. The world has assumed burdens that will bear heavily on all peoples. We shall not escape our share. But whatever may be our trials, however difficult our tasks, they are only the problems of peace, and a victorious peace. The war is over. Whatever the call of duty now we should remember with gratitude that it is nothing compared with the heavy sacrifice so lately made. The genius and fortitude which conquered then cannot now fail.

XXV

STATEMENT ON THE DEATH OF THEODORE ROOSEVELT

THE people of our Commonwealth have learned with profound sorrow of the death of Theodore Roosevelt. No other citizen of the Nation would have brought in so large a degree the feeling of a common loss. During the almost eight years he was President, the people came to see in him a reflection of their ideals of the true Americanism.

He was the advocate of every good cause. He awakened the moral purpose of the Nation and raised the standard of public service. He appealed to the imagination of youth and satisfied the judgment of maturity. In him Massachusetts saw an exponent of her own ideals.

In token of the love and reverence which all the people bore him, I urge that the na-

tional and state flags be flown at half-mast
throughout the Commonwealth until after
his funeral, and that, when next the people
gather for public worship, his loss be marked
with proper ceremony.

XXVI

LINCOLN DAY PROCLAMATION
JANUARY 30, 1919

The Commonwealth of Massachusetts
By His Excellency Calvin Coolidge, Governor

A PROCLAMATION

FIVESCORE and ten years ago that Divine Providence which infinite repetition has made only the more a miracle sent into the world a new life, destined to save a nation. No star, no sign, foretold his coming. About his cradle all was poor and mean save only the source of all great men, the love of a wonderful woman. When she faded way in his tender years, from her deathbed in humble poverty she dowered her son with greatness. There can be no proper observance of a birthday which forgets the mother. Into his origin as into his life men long have looked and wondered. In wisdom great, but in humility greater, in justice strong, but in compassion stronger, he became a leader of men by being a follower of the truth. He overcame evil with good. His presence filled the Nation. He broke the might of oppression. He restored a race to its birthright. His mortal frame has vanished, but his spirit increases with the increasing years, the richest legacy of the greatest century.

Men show by what they worship what they are. It is no accident that before the great example of American manhood our people stand with respect and reverence. And in accordance with this sentiment our laws have provided for a formal recognition of the birthday of Abraham Lincoln, for in him is revealed our ideal, the hope of our country fulfilled.

Now, therefore, by the authority of Massachusetts, the 12th day of February is set apart as

LINCOLN DAY

and its observance recommended as befits the beneficiaries of his life and the admirers of his character, in places of education and worship wherever our people meet one with another.

Given at the Executive Chamber, in Boston, this 30th day of January, in the year of Our Lord one thousand nine hundred and nineteen, and of the independence of the United States of America the one hundred and forty-third.

CALVIN COOLIDGE

By his Excellency the Governor,

ALBERT P. LANGTRY,

Secretary of the Commonwealth.

God save the Commonwealth of Massachusetts.

XXVII

INTRODUCING HENRY CABOT LODGE AND A. LAWRENCE LOWELL AT THE DEBATE ON THE LEAGUE OF NATIONS SYMPHONY HALL
MARCH 19, 1919

WE meet here as representatives of a great people to listen to the discussion of a great question by great men. All America has but one desire, the security of the peace by facts and by parchment which her brave sons have wrought by the sword. It is a duty we owe alike to the living and the dead.

Fortunate is Massachusetts that she has among her sons two men so eminently trained for the task of our enlightenment, a senior Senator of the Commonwealth and the President of a university established in her Constitution. Wherever statesmen gather, wherever men love letters, this day's discussion will be read and pondered. Of these great men in learning, and experience, wise in the science and practice of government, the first to address you is a Senator distinguished at home and famous everywhere — Henry Cabot Lodge.

[After Senator Lodge spoke he introduced President Lowell:]

The next to address you is the President of Harvard University — an educator renowned throughout the world, a learned student of statesmanship, endowed with a wisdom which has made him a leader of men, truly a Master of Arts, eminently a Doctor of Laws, a fitting representative of the Massachusetts domain of letters — Abbott Lawrence Lowell.

XXVIII

VETO OF SALARY INCREASE

To the Honorable Senate and House
  of Representatives:

In accordance with the duty imposed by
the Constitution, a bill entitled, "An act to
establish the compensation of the members
of the General Court," being House No.
1629, is herewith returned without approval.

This bill raises the salaries of members
from $1000 to $1500, an increase of fifty
per cent, and is retroactive. It is necessary
to decide whether the Commonwealth can
well afford this additional tax and whether
any public benefit would accrue from it.

These are times that require careful
scrutiny of public expenditure. The burden
of taxes resulting from war is heavy. The
addition of $142,000 to the expense of the
Commonwealth in perpetuity is not to be
undertaken but upon proven necessity.

Service in the General Court is not oblig-
atory but optional. It is not to be undertaken as a profession or a means of livelihood. It is a voluntary public service. In
accord with the principles of our democratic
institutions a compensation has been given
in order that talent for service rather than
the possession of property might be the
standard of membership. There is no man
of sufficient talent in the Commonwealth
so poor that he cannot serve for a session,
which averages about five months, and five
days each week, at a salary of $1000 —
and travel allowance of $2.50 for each mile
between his home and the State House.
This is too clear for argument. There is no
need to consider those who are too rich to
serve for this sum. It would be futile to discuss whether their services are worth more
or less than this, as that is not here the question. Membership in the General Court is
not a job. There are services rendered to the
Commonwealth by senators and represen-

tatives that are priceless. For the searching out of great principles on which legislation is based there is no adequate compensation. If value for services were the criterion, there would be 280 different salaries. When membership is sought as a means of livelihood, legislation will pass from a public function to a private enterprise. Men do not serve here for pay. They seek work and places of responsibility and find in that seeking, not in their pay, their honor.

The realities of life are not measured by dollars and cents. The skill of the physician, the divine eloquence of the clergyman, the courage of the soldier, that which we call character in all men, are not matters of hire and salary. No person was ever honored for what he received. Honor has been the reward for what he gave. Public acclaim and the ceremonious recognition paid to returning heroes are not on account of their government pay but of the service and sacrifice they gave their country. The place each member of the General Court will hold in the estimation of his constituents will never depend on his salary, but on the ability and integrity with which he does his duty; not on what he receives, but on what he gives; and only out of the bountifulness of his own giving will his constituents raise him to power. Not by indulging himself, but by denying himself, will he reach success.

It is because the General Court has recognized these principles in its past history that it has secured its high place as a legislative body. This act disregards all this and will ever appear to be an undertaking by members to raise their own salaries. The fact that many were thinking of the needs of others will remain unknown. Appearances cannot be disregarded. Those in whom is placed the solemn duty of caring for others ought to think of themselves last or their decisions will lack authority. There is apparent a disposition to deny the disinterestedness and impartiality of government. Such charges are the result of ignorance and an evil desire to destroy our institutions for personal profit. It is of infinite importance to demonstrate that legislation is used not for the benefit of the legislator, but of the public.

The General Court of Massachusetts is a legislative body noted for its fairness and ability. It has no superior. Its critics have for the most part come from the outside and have most frequently been those who have approached it with the purpose of securing selfish desires of their clients or themselves. A long familiarity with it increases respect for it. It is charged with expressing the abiding convictions and conscience of the people of the Commonwealth. The most solemn obligation placed by the Constitution on the Executive is the power to veto its actions. In all matters affecting it the General Court is entitled to his best judgment and carefully considered opinion.

Anything less would be a mark of disrespect and disloyalty to its members. That judgment and opinion, arrived at after a wide counsel with members and others, is here expressed, in the light of an obligation which is not personal, "faithfully and impartially to discharge and perform" the duties of a public office.

XXIX

FLAG DAY PROCLAMATION
MAY 26, 1919

WORKS which endure come from the soul of the people. The mighty in their pride walk alone to destruction. The humble walk hand in hand with Providence to immortality. Their works survive. When the people of the Colonies were defending their liberties against the might of kings, they chose their banner from the design set in the firmament through all eternity. The flags of the great empires of that day are gone, but the Stars and Stripes remain. It pictures the vision of a people whose eyes were turned to the rising dawn. It represents the hope of a father for his posterity. It was never flaunted for the glory of royalty, but to be born under it is to be a child of a king, and to establish a home under it is to be the founder of a royal house. Alone of all flags it expresses the sovereignty of the people which endures when all else passes away. Speaking with their voice it has the sanctity of revelation. He who lives under it and is loyal to it is loyal to truth and justice everywhere. He who lives under it and is disloyal to it is a traitor to the human race everywhere. What could be saved if the flag of the American Nation were to perish?

In recognition of these truths and out of a desire born of a purpose to defend and perpetuate them, the Commonwealth of Massachusetts has by ordinance decreed that for one day of each year their importance should be dwelt upon and remembered. Therefore, in accordance with that authority, the anniversary of the adoption of the national flag, the 14th day of June next, is set apart as

FLAG DAY

and it is earnestly recommended that it be

observed by the people of the Commonwealth by the display of the flag of our
country and in all ways that may testify
to their loyalty and perpetuate its glory.

XXX

AMHERST COLLEGE COMMENCEMENT
June 18, 1919

To the son of any college, although he does not make his connection with his college a profession, a return of Commencement Day recalls many memories. It is likely also, after nearly a quarter of a century, to cause some reflections. It is, I suppose, to give tongue to such memories and reflections that after-dinner speaking is provided. After all due allowance for change of perspective, going to college was a greater event twenty-five years ago than it is to-day. My own memories are not yet ancient enough to warrant their recalling. The greater events of that day are too recent to need to be related.

But I should fail in my duty and neglect my deep conviction if I did not declare that in my day there was no better place to edu-

cate a young man. Most of them came with
a realization that their coming meant a sacrifice at home. They may have lacked a
proficiency in the arts of the drawing room
which sometimes brought a smile; but no
competitor met the Amherst men of that
day on the athletic field or in the post-
graduate school with a smile that did not
soon come off. They had their pranks and
sprees, but they had the ideals of a true
manhood. They were moved with a serious
purpose. He who had less lacked place
among them. They are come and gone from
the campus, those men of the early nineties,
and with them went the power to command.

Those were days that represented especially the spirit of President Seelye. Under
his brilliant and polished successor the Faculty changes were few. There was Professor Wood, the most accomplished intellectual hazer of freshmen. There was Professor
Gibbons, who was strong enough in Greek

derivation so that every second-year man
soon had a clear conception of the meaning
of sophomore. After demonstrating clearly
that on the negative side the derivation of
"contiguity" was not "con" and "tiguity,"
he advised those who could not with equal
clearness demonstrate its derivation on the
positive side to look it up. There were
Morse and Frink, Richardson, Hitchcock,
Estey, Crowell, Tyler, and Garman. All
these and more are gone. The living, no
less eminent, I need not recall. As a teaching force, as an inspirer of youth, for training men how to think, that faculty has had
and will have nowhere any superior.

"So passed that pageant."

The college of to-day has taken on a new
life, a new activity. Military training then
was a spectacle for the Massachusetts Agricultural College. To-day Amherst welcomes
its returning soldiers, and but a little time
since divested itself of the character of a
military camp to resume the wonted garb

of peace. Yet it is and has been the same
institution, — a college of the liberal arts.
In this so-called practical age Amherst has
chosen for her province the most practical
of all, — the culture and the classics of all
time.

Civilization depends not only upon the
knowledge of the people, but upon the use
they make of it. If knowledge be wrong-
fully used, civilization commits suicide.
Broadly speaking, the college is not to educate the individual, but to educate society.
The individual may be ignorant and vicious.
If society have learning and virtue, that
will sustain him. If society lacks learning
and virtue, it perishes. Education must
give not only power but direction. It must
minister to the whole man or it fails.

Such an education considered from the
position of society does not come from science. That provides power alone, but not
direction. Give a savage tribe firearms and
a distillery, and their members will extermi-

nate each other. They have science all right, but misuse it. They lack ideals. These young men that we welcome back with so much pride did not go forth to demonstrate their faith in science. They did not offer their lives because of their belief in any rule of mathematics or any principle of physics or chemistry. The laws of the natural world would be unaffected by their defeat or victory. No; they were defending their ideals, and those ideals came from the classics.

This is preëminently true of the culture of Greece and Rome. Patriotism with them was predominant. Their heroes were those who sacrificed themselves for their country, from the three hundred at Thermopylæ to Horatius at the bridge. Their poets sang of the glory of dying for one's native land. The orations of Demosthenes and Cicero are pitched in the same high strain. The philosophy of Plato and Aristotle and the Greek and Latin classics were the foundation of the

Renaissance. The revival of learning was the revival of Athens and Sparta and of the Imperial City. Modern science is their product. To be included with the classics are modern history and literature, the philosophers, the orators, the statesmen, and poets, — Milton and Shakespeare, Lowell and Whittier, — the Farewell Address, the Reply to Hayne, the Speech at Gettysburg, — it is all these and more that I mean by the classics. They give not only power to the intellect, but direct its course of action.

The classic of all classics is the Bible.

I do not underestimate schools of science and technical arts. They have a high and noble calling in ministering to mankind. They are important and necessary. I am pointing out that in my opinion they do not provide a civilization that can stand without the support of the ideals that come from the classics.

The conclusion to be derived from this position is that a vocational or technical education is not enough. We must have every American citizen well grounded in the classical ideals. Such an education will not unfit him for the work of the world. Did those men in the trenches fight any less valiantly, did they shrink any more from the hardships of war, when a liberal culture had given a broader vision of what the great conflict meant? The discontent in modern industry is the result of a too narrow outlook. A more liberal culture will reveal the importance and nobility of the work of the world, whether in war or peace. It is far from enough to teach our citizens a vocation. Our industrial system will break down unless it is humanized. There is greater need for a liberal culture that will develop the whole man in the whole body of our citizenship. The day when a college education will be the portion of all may not be so far distant as it seems.

We live in a republic. Our Government is exercised through representatives. Their course of action is a very accurate reflection of public opinion. Where shall that be formed and directed unless from the influences, direct and indirect, that come from our institutions of learning. The laws of a republic represent its ideals. They are founded upon public opinion, and public opinion in America up to the present time has drawn its inspiration from the classics. They tell us that Waterloo was won on the football fields of Rugby and Eton. The German war was won by the influence of classical ideals. As a teacher of the classics, as a maker of public opinion, as a source of wise laws, as the herald of a righteous victory, — Amherst College stands on a foundation which has remained unchanged through the ages. May there be in all her sons a conviction that with her abides Him who changes not.

XXXI

HARVARD UNIVERSITY COMMENCE-
MENT
June 19, 1919

No college man who has ever glanced at the Constitution of Massachusetts is likely to miss or forget the generous references there made to Harvard University. It may need a closer study of that instrument, which is older than the American Constitution, to realize the full significance of those most enduring of guaranties that could then be imposed in behalf of Massachusetts institutions.

The convention which framed our Constitution has as its president James Bowdoin, a son of Harvard. He was a man of great strength of character and cast an influence for good upon the deliberations of his day worthy of a place in history more conspicuous than is generally accorded to him. He had as his colleague on the floor no less a person than John Adams. It is not necessary in this presence to designate his alma mater. There were others of importance, but these represented the type of thought that prevailed.

In that noble Declaration of Rights the principles of freedom and equality were first declared. Following this is set forth the right of religious liberty and the duty of citizens to support places of religious worship and instruction; and in the Frame of Government, after establishing the University, there is given to legislators and magistrates a mandate forever to cherish and support the cause of education and institutions of learning. These were the declaration of broad and liberal policies. They are capable of being combined, for in fact they declare that teaching, whether it be by clergy or laity, is of an importance that requires it to be surrounded with the same safeguards and guaranties as freedom and equality. In fact the Constitution declares that "wisdom and knowledge, as well as virtue, diffused generally among the body of the people, are necessary for the preservation of their rights and liberties." John Adams and James Bowdoin knew that freedom was the fruit of knowledge. Their conclusions were drawn from the directions of Holy Writ — "Come, know the truth, and it shall make you free."

These principles there laid down with so much solemnity have now the same binding force as in those revolutionary days when they were recognized and proclaimed. I am not unaware that they are old. Whatever is, is old. It is but our own poor apprehension of it that is new. It would be well if they were re-apprehended. It is not well if the great diversity of modern learning has made the truth so little of a novelty that it lacks all reverence.

The days of the Revolution were days of reverence and of applied reverence. Teaching was to a considerable extent in the hands of the clergy. Institutions of learning were presided over by clergymen. The teacher spoke with the voice of authority. He was treated with deference. He held a place in the community that was not only secure but high. The rewards of his services were comparatively large. He was a leader of the people. From him came the inspiration of liberty. It was in the meeting-houses that the Revolution was framed.

This dual character little exists now, but the principle is the same. Teaching is the same high calling, but how lacking now in comparative appreciation. The compensation of many teachers and clergymen is far less than the pay of unskilled labor. The salaries of college professors are much less than like training and ability would command in the commercial world. We pay a good price to bank men to guard our money. We compensate liberally the manufacturer and the merchant; but we fail to appreciate those who guard the minds of our youth or those who preside over our congregations. We have lost our reverence for the profession of teaching and bestowed it upon the profession of acquiring.

This will have such a reaction as might be expected. Some of the clergy, seeing their own rewards are disproportionate, will draw the conclusion that all rewards are disproportionate, that the whole distribution of wealth is unsound; and turn to a belief in and an advocacy of some kind of a socialistic state. Some of our teachers, out of a like discontent, will listen too willingly to revolutionary doctrines which have not originated in meeting-houses but are the importations of those who lack nothing but the power to destroy all that our civilization holds dear. Unless these conditions are changed, these professions will not attract to their services young men of the same comparative quality of ability and character that in the past they commanded.

In our pursuit of prosperity we have forgotten and neglected its foundations. It is true that many of our institutions of learning are well endowed and have spacious buildings, but the plant is not enough. Many modern schoolhouses put to shame any public buildings that were erected in the Colonies. I am directing attention to the comparative position of the great mass of teachers and clergymen. They are not properly appreciated or properly paid. They have provided the foundations of our liberties. The importance of their position cannot be overestimated. They have been faithful though neglected; but a state which neglects or refuses to support any class will soon find that such class neglects and refuses to support it. The remedy lies in part with private charity, in part with government action; but it lies wholly with public opinion. Private charity must worthily support its clergymen and the faculty and instructors of our higher institutions of learning; and the Government must adequately reward the teachers in its schools. In the great bound forward which has been taken in a material way, these two noble professions, the pillars of liberty and equality, have been neglected and left behind. They must be reëstablished. They must be restored to the place of reverence they formerly held.

The profession of teaching has come down to us with a sanction of antiquity greater than all else. So far back as we can peer into human history there has stood a priesthood that has led its people intellectually and morally. Teaching is leading. The fundamental needs of humanity do not change. They are constant. These influences so potent in the development of Massachusetts cannot be exchanged for a leadership that is bred of the market-place, to her advantage. We must turn our eyes from what is to what ought to be. The men of the day of John Adams and James Bowdoin had a vision that looked into the heart of things. They led a revolution that swept on to a successful conclusion. They established a nation that has endured until its flag is the ancient among the banners of the earth. Their counsel will not be mocked. The men of that day almost alone in history brought a Revolution to its objective. Not only that, they reached it in such a condition that it there remained. The counter-attack of disorder failed entirely to dislodge it. Their success lay entirely in the convictions they had. No nation can reject these convictions and remain a republic. Anarchy or despotism will overwhelm it.

Massachusetts established Harvard College to be a defender of righteous convictions, of reverence for truth and for the heralds of truth. The purpose set forth in the Constitution is clear and plain. It recognizes with the clear conviction of men not thinking of themselves that the cause of America is the cause of education, but of education with a soul, a trained intellect but guided ever by an enlightened conscience. We of our day need to recognize with the same vision that when these fail, America has failed.

XXXII

PLYMOUTH, LABOR DAY
SEPTEMBER 1, 1919

THE laws of our country have designated the first Monday of each September as Labor Day. It is truly an American day, for it was here that for the first time in history a government was founded on a recognition of the sovereignty of the citizen which has irresistibly led to a realization of the dignity of his occupation. It is with added propriety that this day is observed this year. For the first time in five years it comes at a time when the issue of world events makes it no longer doubtful whether the American conception of work as the crowning glory of men free and equal is to prevail over the age-old European conception that work is the badge of the menial and the inferior. The American ideal has prevailed on European battle-fields through the loyalty, devotion, and sacrifice of American labor.

The duty of citizenship in this hour is to strive to maintain and extend that ideal at home.

The past five years have been a time of rapid change and great progress for the American people. Not only have the hours and conditions of labor been greatly improved, but wages have increased about one hundred per cent. There has been a great economic change for the better among all wage-earners.

We have known that political power was with the people, because they have the votes. We have generally supposed that economic power was not with the people, because they did not own the property. This supposition, probably never true, is growing more and more to be contrary to the facts. The great outstanding fact in the economic life of America is that the wealth of the Nation is owned by the people of the Nation. The stockholders of the great corporations run into the hundreds of thousands, the small tradesmen, the thrifty householders, the tillers of the soil, the depositors in savings banks, and the now owners of government bonds, make a number that includes nearly our entire people. This would be illustrated by a few Massachusetts examples from figures which were reported in 1918:

Number of Stockholders

Railroads..................	40,485
Street railways	17,527
Telephone	49,688
Western Union Telegraph...	9,360
	117,060

Number of Employees

Railroads..................	20,604
Street railways	25,000
Telephone................	11,471
Western Union Telegraph...	2,065
	59,140

Savings bank depositors. ...	2,491,646
Railroad, street railway, and telephone bonds held by savings banks and savings departments of trust companies..................	$267,795,636
Savings bank deposits	$1,022,342,583

Money is pouring into savings banks at the rate of $275,000 each working day.

Comment on these figures is unnecessary. There is, of course, some reduplication, but in these four public service enterprises there are in Massachusetts almost twice as many direct owners as there are employees. Two persons out of three have money in the savings bank — men, women, and children. There is this additional fact: more than one quarter of the stupendous sum of over a billion dollars of the savings of nearly two and a half million savings depositors is invested in railroad, street railway, and telephone securities.

With these examples in mind it would appear that our problem of economic justice in Massachusetts, where we live and for which alone we can legislate, is not quite so simple as assuming that we can take from one class and give to another class. We are reaching and maintaining the position in this Commonwealth where the property class and the employed class are not separate, but identical. There is a relationship of interdependence which makes their interests the same in the long run. Most of us earn our livelihood through some form of employment. More and more of our people are in possession of some part of the wages of yesterday, and so are investors. This is the ideal economic condition.

The great aim of our Government is to protect the weak — to aid them to become strong. Massachusetts is an industrial State. If her people prosper, it must be by that means in some of its broad avenues. How can our people be made strong? Only as they draw their strength from our industries. How can they do that? Only by building up our industries and making them strong. This is fundamental. It is the place to begin. These are the instruments of all our achievement. When they fail, all fails. When they prosper, all prosper. Workmen's compensation, hours and conditions of labor are cold consolations, if there be no employment. And employment can be had only if some one finds it profitable. The greater the profit, the greater the wages.

This is one of the economic lessons of the war. It should be remembered now when taxes are to be laid, and in the period of readjustment. Taxes must be measured by the ability to meet them out of surplus income. Industry must expand or fail. It must show a surplus after all payments of wages, taxes, and returns to investors. Conscription can call once, then all is over. Just requirements can be met again and again with ever-increasing ability.

Justice and the general welfare go hand in hand. Government had to take over our transportation interests in order to do such justice to them that they could pay their employees and carry our merchandise. They have been so restricted lest they do harm that they became unable to do good. Their surplus was gone, and we New Englanders had to go without coal. Seeing now more clearly than before the true interests of wage-earner, investor, and the public, which is the consumer, we shall hereafter be willing to pay the price and secure the benefits of justice to all these coördinate interests.

We have met the economic problem of the returning service men. They have been assimilated into our industrial life with little delay and with no disturbance of existing conditions. The day of adversity has passed. The American people met and overcame it. The day of prosperity has come. The great question now is whether the American people can endure their prosperity. I believe they can. The power to preserve America is in the same hands to-day that it was when the German army was almost at the gates of Paris. That power is with the people themselves; not one class, but all classes; not one occupation, but all occupations; not one citizen, but all citizens.

During the past five years we have heard

many false prophets. Some were honest, but unwise; some plain slackers; a very few were simply public enemies. Had their counsels prevailed, America would have been destroyed. In general they appealed to the lower impulses of the people, for in their ignorance they believed the most powerful motive of this Nation was a sodden selfishness. They said the war would never affect us; we should confine ourselves to making money. They argued for peace at any price. They opposed selective service. They sought to prevent sending soldiers to Europe. They advocated peace by negotiation. They were answered from beginning to end by the loyalty of the American workingmen and the wisdom of their leaders. That loyalty and that wisdom will not desert us now. The voices that would have lured us to destruction were unheeded. All counsels of selfishness were unheeded, and America responded with a spirit which united our people as never before to the call of duty.

Having accomplished this great task, having emerged from the war the strongest, the least burdened nation on earth, are we now to fail before our lesser task? Are we to turn aside from the path that has led us to success? Who now will set selfishness above duty? The counsel that Samuel Gompers gave is still sound, when he said in effect, "America may not be perfect. It has the imperfections of all things human. But it is the best country on earth, and the man who will not work for it, who will not fight for it, and if need be die for it, is unworthy to live in it."

Happily, the day when the call to fight or die is now past. But the day when it is the duty of all Americans to work will remain forever. Our great need now is for more of everything for everybody. It is not money that the nation or the world needs to-day, but the products of labor. These products are to be secured only by the united efforts of an entire people. The trained business man and the humblest workman must each contribute. All of us must work, and in that work there should be no interruption. There must be more food, more clothing, more shelter. The directors of industry must direct it more efficiently, the workers in industry must work in it more efficiently. Such a course saved us in war; only such a course can preserve us in peace. The power to preserve America, with all that it now means to the world, all the great hope that it holds for humanity, lies in the hands of the people. Talents and opportunity exist. Application only is uncertain. May Labor Day of 1919 declare with an increased emphasis the resolution of all Americans to work for America.

XXXIII

WESTFIELD

September 3, 1919

We come here on this occasion to honor the past, and in that honor render more secure the present. It was by such men as settled Westfield, and two hundred and fifty years ago established by law a chartered and ordered government, that the foundations of Massachusetts were laid. And it was on the foundations of Massachusetts that there began that training of the people for the great days that were to come, when they were prepared to endorse and support the principles set out in the Declaration of Independence, the Constitution of the United States of America, and the Emancipation Proclamation of Abraham Lincoln. Here were planted the same seeds of righteousness victorious which later flourished with such abundance at Saratoga, at Gettysburg, and at the second battle of the Marne. Stupendous results, the product of a people working with an everlasting purpose.

While celebrating the history of Westfield, this day has been set apart to the memory of one of her most illustrious sons, General William Shepard. To others are assigned the history of your town and the biography of your soldier. Into those particulars I shall not enter. But the principles of government and of citizenship which they so well represent, and nobly illustrate, will never be untimely or unworthy of reiteration.

The political history of Westfield has seen the success of a great forward movement, to which it contributed its part, in establishing the principle, that the individual in his rights is supreme, and that "governments derive their just powers from the consent of the governed." It is the establishment of liberty, under an ordered form of government, in this ancient town, by the people themselves, that to-day draws us here in admiration of her achievements. When we turn to the life of her patriot son we see that he no less grandly illustrated the principle, that to such government, so established, the people owe an allegiance which has the binding power of the most solemn obligation.

There is such a disposition in these days to deny that our Government was formed by, or is now in control of, the people, that a glance at the history of the days of General Shepard is peculiarly pertinent and instructive.

The Constitution of Massachusetts, with its noble Declaration of Rights, was adopted in 1780. Under it we still live with scarce any changes that affect the rights of the people. The end of the Revolutionary War was 1783. Shays's Rebellion was in 1787. The American Constitution was ratified and adopted in 1788. These dates tell us what the form of government was in this period.

If there are any who doubt that our institutions, formed in those days, did not establish a peoples' government, let them study the action of the Massachusetts Convention which ratified the Federal Constitution in 1788. Presiding over it was the popular patriot Governor John Hancock. On the floor sat Samuel Adams, who had been the father of the Revolution, preëminent champion of the liberty of the people. Such an influence had he, that his assertion of satisfaction, was enough to carry the delegates. Like a majority of the members he came opposed to ratification. Having totally thrown off the authority of foreign power, they came suspicious of all outside authority. Besides there were eighteen members who had taken part in Shays's Rebellion, so hostile were they to the execution of all law. Mr. Adams was finally convinced by a gathering of the workingmen among his constituents, who exercised their constitutional right of instructing their rep-

resentatives. Their opinion was presented
to him by Paul Revere. "How many me-
chanics were at the Green Dragon when
these resolutions were passed?" asked Mr.
Adams. "More, sir, than the Green Dragon
could hold." "And where were the rest?"
"In the streets, sir." "And how many were
in the streets?" "More than there are stars
in the sky." This is supposed to have convinced the great Massachusetts tribune that
it was his duty to support ratification.

There were those, however, who distrusted the Constitution and distrusted its
proponents. They viewed lawyers and men
of means with great jealousy. Amos Singletary expressed their sentiments in the
form of an argument that has not ceased
to be repeated in the discussion of all
public affairs. "These lawyers," said he,
"and men of learning and moneyed men
that talk so finely and gloss over matters
so smoothly, to make us poor illiterates
swallow the pill, expect to get into Con-

gress themselves. They mean to be managers of the Constitution. They mean to
get all the money into their hands and
then they will swallow up us little folk, like
the great Leviathan, Mr. President: yes,
just like the whale swallowed up Jonah."
In the convention sat Jonathan Smith,
a farmer from Lanesboro. He had seen
Shays's Rebellion in Berkshire. There had
been no better example of a man of the
people desiring the common good.

"I am a plain man," said Mr. Smith,
"and am not used to speak in public, but
I am going to show the effects of anarchy,
that you may see why I wish for good government. Last winter people took up arms,
and then, if you went to speak to them, you
had the musket of death presented to your
breast. They would rob you of your property,
threaten to burn your houses, oblige you
to be on your guard night and day. Alarms
spread from town to town, families were
broken up; the tender mother would cry,

'Oh, my son is among them! What shall I do for my child?' Some were taken captive; children taken out of their schools and carried away. . . . How dreadful was this! Our distress was so great that we should have been glad to snatch at anything that looked like a government. . . . Now, Mr. President, when I saw this Constitution, I found that it was a cure for these disorders. I got a copy of it, and read it over and over. . . . I did not go to any lawyer, to ask his opinion; we have no lawyer in our town, and we do well enough without. My honourable old daddy there (pointing to Mr. Singletary) won't think that I expect to be a Congressman, and swallow up the liberties of the people. I never had any post, nor do I want one. But I don't think the worse of the Constitution because lawyers, and men of learning, and moneyed men are fond of it. I am not of such a jealous make. They that are honest men themselves are not apt to suspect other people. . . . Brother farmers, let us suppose a case, now. Suppose you had a farm of 50 acres, and your title was disputed, and there was a farm of 5000 acres joined to you that belonged to a man of learning, and his title was involved in the same difficulty; would you not be glad to have him for your friend, rather than to stand alone in the dispute? Well, the case is the same. These lawyers, these moneyed men, these men of learning, are all embarked in the same cause with us, and we must all sink or swim together. Shall we throw the Constitution overboard because it does not please us all alike? Suppose two or three of you had been at the pains to break up a piece of rough land and sow it with wheat: would you let it lie waste because you could not agree what sort of a fence to make? Would it not be better to put up a fence that did not please every one's fancy, rather than keep disputing about it until the wild beasts came in and devoured the crop? Some gentlemen say,

Don't be in a hurry; take time to consider. I say, There is a time to sow and a time to reap. We sowed our seed when we sent men to the Federal Convention, now is the time to reap the fruit of our labour; and if we do not do it now, I am afraid we shall never have another opportunity."

There spoke the common sense of the common man of the Commonwealth. The counsel of the farmer from the country, joined with the resolutions of the working-men from the city, carried the convention and the Constitution was ratified. In the light of succeeding history, who shall say, that it was not the voice of the people, speaking with the voice of Infinite Author-ity?

The attitude of Samuel Adams, William Shepard, Jonathan Smith and the working-men of Boston toward government, is wor-thy of our constant emulation. They had not hesitated to take up arms against tyr-anny in the Revolution, but having established a government of the people they were equally determined to defend and support it. They hated the usurper whether king, or Parliament, or mob, but they bowed before the duly constituted authority of the people.

When the question of pardoning the convicted leaders of the rebellion came up, Adams opposed it. "In monarchies," he said, "the crime of treason and rebellion may admit of being pardoned or lightly punished; but the man who dares to rebel against the laws of a republic ought to suffer death." We are all glad mercy prevailed and pardon was granted. But the calm judgment of Samuel Adams, the lover of liberty, "the man of the town meeting" whose clear vision, taught by bitter experience, saw that all usurpation is tyranny, must not go unheeded now. The authority of a just government derived from the consent of the governed, has back of it a Power that does not fail.

All wars bring in their trail great hardships. They existed in the day of General
Shepard. They exist now. Having set up a
sound government in Massachusetts, having
secured their independence, as the result of
a victorious war, the people expected a sea-
son of easy prosperity. In that they were
temporarily disappointed. Some rebelling,
were overthrown. The adoption of the Federal Constitution brought relief and prosperity.

Success has attended the establishment
here of a government of the people. We of
this day have just finished a victorious war
that has added new glory to American arms.
We are facing some hardships, but they are
not serious. Private obligations are not so
large as to be burdensome. Taxes can be
paid. Prosperity abounds. But the great
promise of the future lies in the loyalty and
devotion of the people to their own Government. They are firm in the conviction of the
fathers, that liberty is increased only by

increasing the determination to support a government of the people, as established in this ancient town, and defended by its patriotic sons.

XXXIV

*The Commonwealth of Massachusetts
By His Excellency Calvin Coolidge, Governor*

A PROCLAMATION

THE entire State Guard of Massachusetts
has been called out. Under the Constitution
the Governor is the Commander-in-Chief
thereof by an authority of which he could
not if he chose divest himself. That command I must and will exercise. Under the
law I hereby call on all the police of Boston
who have loyally and in a never-to-be-for-
gotten way remained on duty to aid me in
the performance of my duty of the restora-
tion and maintenance of order in the city
of Boston, and each of such officers is required to act in obedience to such orders as
I may hereafter issue or cause to be issued.

I call on every citizen to aid me in the
maintenance of law and order.

Given at the Executive Chamber, in Boston, this
eleventh day of September, in the year of our Lord

one thousand nine hundred and nineteen, and of the Independence of the United States of America the one hundred and forty-fourth.

CALVIN COOLIDGE

By His Excellency the Governor,
ALBERT P. LANGTRY
Secretary of the Commonwealth

God save the Commonwealth of Massachusetts.

XXXV

AN ORDER

To EDWIN U. CURTIS,

As you are Police Commissioner of the City of Boston,

Executive Order No. 1

You are hereby directed, for the purpose of assisting me in the performance of my duty, pursuant to the proclamation issued by me this day, to proceed in the performance of your duties as Police Commissioner of the city of Boston under my command and in obedience to such orders as I shall issue from time to time, and obey only such orders as I may so issue or transmit.

CALVIN COOLIDGE
Governor of Massachusetts

XXXVI

A TELEGRAM

BOSTON, MASS., *Sept.* 14, 1919

MR. SAMUEL GOMPERS

President American Federation of Labor, New York City, N.Y.

Replying to your telegram, I have already refused to remove the Police Commissioner of Boston. I did not appoint him. He can assume no position which the courts would uphold except what the people have by the authority of their law vested in him. He speaks only with their voice. The right of the police of Boston to affiliate has always been questioned, never granted, is now prohibited. The suggestion of President Wilson to Washington does not apply to Boston. There the police have remained on duty. Here the Policemen's Union left their duty, an action which President Wilson characterized as a crime against civilization. Your assertion that the Commissioner was wrong cannot justify the wrong of leaving the city unguarded. That furnished the opportunity, the criminal element furnished the action. There is no right to strike against the public safety by anybody, anywhere, any time. You ask that the public safety again be placed in the hands of these same policemen while they continue in disobedience to the laws of Massachusetts and in their refusal to obey the orders of the Police Department. Nineteen men have been tried and removed. Others having abandoned their duty, their places have, under the law, been declared vacant on the opinion of the Attorney-General. I can suggest no authority outside the courts to take further action. I wish to join and assist in taking a broad view of every situation. A grave responsibility rests on all of us. You can depend on me to support you in every legal action and sound policy. I am equally determined to defend the sovereignty of Massachusetts and to maintain the authority and jurisdiction over her public officers where it has been placed by the Constitution and law of her people.

CALVIN COOLIDGE
Governor of Massachusetts

XXXVII

The Commonwealth of Massachusetts
By His Excellency Calvin Coolidge, Governor

A PROCLAMATION

THERE appears to be a misapprehension as to the position of the police of Boston. In the deliberate intention to intimidate and coerce the Government of this Commonwealth a large body of policemen, urging all others to join them, deserted their posts of duty, letting in the enemy. This act of theirs was voluntary, against the advice of their well wishers, long discussed and premeditated, and with the purpose of obstructing the power of the Government to protect its citizens or even to maintain its own existence. Its success meant anarchy. By this act through the operation of the law they dispossessed themselves. They went out of office. They stand as though they had never been appointed.

Other police remained on duty. They are the real heroes of this crisis. The State Guard responded most efficiently. Thousands have volunteered for the Guard and the Militia. Money has been contributed from every walk of life by the hundreds of thousands for the encouragement and relief of these loyal men. These acts have been spontaneous, significant, and decisive. I propose to support all those who are supporting their own Government with every power which the people have entrusted to me.

There is an obligation, inescapable, no less solemn, to resist all those who do not support the Government. The authority of the Commonwealth cannot be intimidated or coerced. It cannot be compromised. To place the maintenance of the public security in the hands of a body of men who have attempted to destroy it would be to flout the sovereignty of the laws the people have made. It is my duty to resist any such proposal. Those who would counsel it join hands with those whose acts have threatened to destroy the Government. There is no middle ground. Every attempt to prevent the formation of a new police force is a blow at the Government. That way treason lies. No man has a right to place his own ease or convenience or the opportunity of making money above his duty to the State.

This is the cause of all the people. I call on every citizen to stand by me in executing the oath of my office by supporting the authority of the Government and resisting all assaults upon it.

Given at the Executive Chamber, in Boston, this twenty-fourth day of September, in the year of our Lord one thousand nine hundred and nineteen, and of the Independence of the United States of America the one hundred and forty-fourth.

CALVIN COOLIDGE

By His Excellency the Governor,

HERBERT H. BOYNTON
Deputy, Acting Secretary of the Commonwealth

God save the Commonwealth of Massachusetts.

XXXVIII

HOLY CROSS COLLEGE
June 25, 1919

To come from the press of public affairs, where the practical side of life is at its flood, into these calm and classic surroundings, where ideals are cherished for their own sake, is an intense relief and satisfaction. Even in the full flow of Commencement exercises it is apparent that here abide the truth and the servants of the truth. Here appears the fulfillment of the past in the grand company of alumni, recalling a history already so thick with laurels. Here is the hope of the future, brighter yet in the young men to-day sent forth.

"The unarmed youth of heaven. But o'er their heads
Celestial armory, shield, helm and spear,
Hung bright, with diamond flaming and with gold."

In them the dead past lives. They represent the college. They are the college. It is

not in the campus with its imposing halls
and temples, nor in the silent lore of the
vast library or the scientific instruments of
well-equipped laboratories, but in the men
who are the incarnation of all these, that
your college lives. It is not enough that
there be knowledge, history and poetry,
eloquence and art, science and mathematics, philosophy and ethics, ideas and ideals.
They must be vitalized. They must be fash-
ioned into life. To send forth men who live
all these is to be a college. This temple of
learning must be translated into human
form if it is to exercise any influence over
the affairs of mankind, or if its alumni are
to wield the power of education.

A great thinker and master of the expression of thought has told us:

"It was before Deity, embodied in a human form, walking among men, partaking
of their infirmities, leaning on their bosoms,
weeping over their graves, slumbering in
the manger, bleeding on the cross, that

the prejudices of the Synagogue, and the doubts of the Academy, and the pride of the Portico, and the fasces of the Lictor, and the swords of thirty Legions, were humbled in the dust."

If college-bred men are to exercise the influence over the progress of the world which ought to be their portion, they must exhibit in their lives a knowledge and a learning which is marked with candor, humility, and the honest mind.

The present is ever influenced mightily by the past. Patrick Henry spoke with great wisdom when he declared to the Continental Congress, "I have but one lamp by which my feet are guided and that is the lamp of experience." Mankind is finite. It has the limits of all things finite. The processes of government are subject to the same limitations, and, lacking imperfections, would be something more than human. It is always easy to discover flaws, and, pointing them out, to criticize. It is

not so easy to suggest substantial remedies
or propose constructive policies. It is characteristic of the unlearned that they are forever proposing something which is old, and,
because it has recently come to their own
attention, supposing it to be new. Into this
error men of liberal education ought not to
fall. The forms and processes of government are not new. They have been known,
discussed, and tried in all their varieties
through the past ages. That which America
exemplifies in her Constitution and system of representative government is the
most modern, and of any yet devised gives
promise of being the most substantial and
enduring.

It is not unusual to hear arguments
against our institutions and our Government, addressed particularly to recent arrivals and the sons of recent arrivals to our
shores. They sometimes take the form of a
claim that our institutions were founded
long ago; that changed conditions require

that they now be changed. Especially is it
claimed by those seeking such changes that
these new arrivals and men of their race
and ideas had no hand in the making of our
country, and that it was formed by those
who were hostile to them and therefore they
owe it no support. Whatever may be the
condition in relation to others, and whatever ignorance and bigotry may imagine,
such arguments do not apply to those of the
race and blood so prominent in this assemblage. To establish this it were but necessary to cite eleven of the fifty-five signers of
the Declaration of Independence and recall that on the roll of Washington's generals were Sullivan, Knox, Wayne, and the
gallant son of Trinity College, Dublin, who
fell at Quebec at the head of his troops, —
Richard Montgomery. But scholarship has
answered ignorance. The learned and patriotic research of men of the education of
Dr. James J. Walsh and Michael J. O'Brien,
the historian of the Irish American Society,

has demonstrated that a generous portion of the rank and file of the men who fought in the Revolution and supported those who framed our institutions was not alien to those who are represented here. It is no wonder that from among such that which is American has drawn some of its most steadfast defenders.

In these days of violent agitation scholarly men should reflect that the progress of the past has been accomplished not by the total overthrow of institutions so much as by discarding that which was bad and preserving that which was good; not by revolution but by evolution has man worked out his destiny. We shall miss the central feature of all progress unless we hold to that process now. It is not a question of whether our institutions are perfect. The most beneficent of our institutions had their beginnings in forms which would be particularly odious to us now. Civilization began with war and slavery; government began in absolute despotism; and religion itself grew out of superstition which was oftentimes marked with human sacrifices. So out of our present imperfections we shall develop that which is more perfect. But the candid mind of the scholar will admit and seek to remedy all wrongs with the same zeal with which it defends all rights.

From the knowledge and the learning of the scholar there ought to be developed an abiding faith. What is the teaching of all history? That which is necessary for the welfare and progress of the human race has never been destroyed. The discoverers of truth, the teachers of science, the makers of inventions, have passed to their last rewards, but their works have survived. The Phœnician galleys and the civilization which was born of their commerce have perished, but the alphabet which that people perfected remains. The shepherd kings of Israel, the temple and empire of Solomon, have gone the way of all the earth, but the Old Testament has been preserved for the inspiration of mankind. The ark of the covenant and the seven-pronged candle-stick have passed from human view; the inhabitants of Judea have been dispersed to the ends of the earth, but the New Testament has survived and increased in its influence among men. The glory of Athens and Sparta, the grandeur of the Imperial City, are a long-lost memory, but the poetry of Homer and Virgil, the oratory of Demosthenes and Cicero, the philosophy of Plato and Aristotle, abide with us forevermore. Whatever America holds that may be of value to posterity will not pass away.

The long and toilsome processes which have marked the progress of the past cannot be shunned by the present generation to our advantage. We have no right to expect as our portion something substantially different from human experience in the past. The constitution of the universe does not change. Human nature remains constant. That service and sacrifice which have been the price of past progress are the price of progress now.

This is not a gospel of despair, but of hope and high expectation. Out of many tribulations mankind has pressed steadily onward. The opportunity for a rational existence was never before so great. Blessings were never so bountiful. But the evidence was never so overwhelming as now that men and nations must live rationally or perish.

The defenses of our Commonwealth are not material but mental and spiritual. Her fortifications, her castles, are her institutions of learning. Those who are admitted to the college campus tread the ramparts of the State. The classic halls are the armories from which are furnished forth the knights in armor to defend and support our liberty. For such high purpose has Holy

Cross been called into being. A firm foundation of the Commonwealth. A defender of righteousness. A teacher of holy men. Let her turrets continue to rise, showing forth "the way, the truth and the light" —

"In thoughts sublime that pierce the night like stars,
And with their mild persistence urge man's arch
To vaster issues."

XXXIX

REPUBLICAN STATE CONVENTION
TREMONT TEMPLE, BOSTON
OCTOBER 4, 1919

ANCIENT custom crystallized to law has drawn us here. We come to renew our pledge publicly at the altar of our country. We come in the light of history and of reason. We come to take counsel both from experience and from imagination. Over us shines a glorious past, before us lies a promising future. Around us is a renewed determination deep and solemn that this Commonwealth of ours shall endure.

The period since our last election has been one of momentous events. Within its first week the victorious advance of America and her allies terminated in the armistice of November eleventh. The power of organized despotisms had been proven to be inferior to the power of organized republics. Reason had again triumphed over absolutism. The "still small voice" of the moral law was seen to be greater than the might of kings. The world appeal to duty triumphed over the world appeal to selfishness. It always will. There will be far-reaching results from all this which no one can now foresee. But some things are apparent. The power of the people has been revealed. The worth of the individual man shines forth with an increased glory. But most significant of all, for it lies at the foundation of all civilization and all progress, was the demonstration that the citizens of the great republics of the earth possess the power which they dare to use, of maintaining among all men the orderly processes of revealed law.

These are no new doctrines in Massachusetts. For nearly three hundred years she has laid her course according to these principles, extending the blessings which arise from them to her citizens, ever ready to defend them with her treasure and her blood. In this the past year has been no exception.

In recognition of the long-established policy of making this Commonwealth first in humanitarian legislation, the General Court enacted a law providing for reducing a fifty-four hour week for women and minors to a forty-eight hour week. It passed the weavers' specification bill. The allowance under the workmen's compensation law was increased. Local option was provided on the question of a twelve-hour day for firemen. Authority was granted corporations to give their employees a voice in their management. Representatives of the employees have been appointed to the Board of Trustees of great public service corporations. Profiteering has been made a crime. A special commission of which the chairman is Brigadier-General John H. Sherburne was established to deal with the problem of the high cost of living — with power which has been effective in reducing the prices of the necessaries of life. No other State has taken any effective measure. The compensation of public employees has been increased. The entire public service of the Commonwealth has been reorganized in accordance with the constitutional amendment into twenty departments. In caring for her service men Massachusetts led all the States of the Nation in relief and in assistance, besides voting the stupendous sum of twenty million dollars, not as compensation, but as recognition of the gratitude due those who had represented us in the great war. The educational opportunities of the youth of the State have been improved. All of these acts of great importance, which are of course only representative of the character of current legislation, had the executive approval. There has been not only a sympathetic but a very practical attitude toward the ideal expressed in my inaugural address, that there is a right to be well born, well reared, well educated, well employed, and well paid. We shall not be shaken in the mature determination to promote these policies. The ancient faith of Massachusetts in the worth of her citizens, the cause of great solicitude for the welfare of each individual, will remain undiminished.

The many uncertainties in transportation which are State, Nation, and world wide, sent our street railway problems to an expert commission which will report to a special session of the General Court. It is recognized that the rate of fare necessary to pay for the service rendered has in some instances become prohibitive. Some roads and portions of roads have been closed down. There must be relief. But such relief must be in accord with sound economic principles. What the public has the public must pay for. From this there is no escape. Under private, or public, ownership or operation this rule will be the same. We must face the facts and restore this necessary service to the people in such a form that they can meet its costs. In meeting this issue, not hysterically, not with demagogy, but calmly, with candor, applying an adequate remedy to ascertained facts, Massachusetts, as usual, will lead all the other States of the Nation.

That agitation and unrest which has been characteristic of the whole world since the close of the war has had some manifestations here. There is a natural desire in every human mind to seek better conditions. Such a desire is altogether praiseworthy. There must, however, be discrimination in the methods employed. Wholesale criticism of everybody and everything does not necessarily exhibit statesmanlike qualities, and may not be true. Not all those who are working to better the condition of the people are Bolsheviki or enemies of society. Not all those who are attempting to conduct a successful business are profiteers.

But unreasonable criticism and agitation for unreasonable remedies will avail nothing. We, in common with the whole world, are suffering from a shortage of materials. There is but one remedy for this, increased production. We need to use sparingly what we have and make more. No progress will be made by shouting Bolsheviki and profiteers. What we need is thrift and industry. Let everybody keep at work. Profitable employment is the death blow to Bolshevism and abundant production is disaster to the profiteer. Our salvation lies in putting forth greater effort, in manfully assuming our own burdens, rather than in entertaining the pleasing delusion that they can be shifted to some other shoulders. Those who attempt to lead people on in this expectation only add to their burdens and their dangers.

The people of Boston have recently seen the result of agitation and unrest in its police force. The policy of that department, established by an order of former Commissioner O'Meara and adopted by a rule which has the force of law by the present Commissioner Curtis, prohibited a police union from affiliating with an outside union. In spite of this such a union was formed and persisted in with acknowledged and open defiance of the rules and of the counsel and almost entreaties of the officers of the department. Such disobedience continuing, the leaders were cited for trial on charges and heard with their counsel before the Commissioner. After thorough consideration, and opportunity again to obey the rules, they were found guilty. In order to give a chance to recant sentence was suspended. Shortly after, three fourths of the police force abandoned their posts and refused further to perform their duties. During the next few hours, there was destruction of property in the city but happily no loss of life.

Meantime there had been various efforts

to save the situation. Some urged me to remove the Commissioner, some to request him to alter his course. To all these I had to reply that I had no authority whatever over his actions and could not lawfully interfere with him. It was my duty to support him in the execution of the law and that I should do. I was glad to confer with any one and give my help where it was sought. The Commissioner was appointed by my predecessor in office for a term of years. I could with almost equal propriety interfere in the decisions of the Supreme Court.

To restore order, I at once and by prearrangement with him and the Commissioner, offered to the Mayor to call out the State Guard. At his request I did so, immediately beginning restoring obedience to the law. On account of the public danger, I called on the Commissioner to aid me in the execution of my duties of keeping order, and issued a proclamation to that effect.

To various suggestions that the police be permitted to return I replied that the Attorney-General had ruled that by law that could not be done and while I had no power to appoint, discharge, or reinstate, I was opposed to placing the public security again in the keeping of this body of men. There is an obligation to forgive but it does not extend to the unrepentant. To give them aid and comfort is to support their evil doing and to become what is known in law as an accessory after the fact. A government which does that is a reproach to civilization and will soon have on its hands the blood of its citizens.

The response to the appeal to support the Government of Massachusetts in sustaining law and order was instantaneous. It came from the State Guard, from volunteers for police, and the militia, from contributions gathered among all classes now reaching hundreds of thousands of dollars, from the loyal police of Boston, from all quarters of the Commonwealth and beyond. These forces may all be dissipated, they may be defeated, but while I am entrusted with the office of their Commander-in-Chief they will not be surrendered. Over them and over every other law-abiding citizen has gone up the white flag of Massachusetts. Who is there that by compromising the authority of her laws dares to haul down that flag? I have resisted and propose to continue in resistance to such action.

This issue is perfectly plain. The Government of Massachusetts is not seeking to resist the lawful action or sound policy of organized labor. It has time and again passed laws for the protection and encouragement of trade unions. It has done so under my administration upon my recommendation to a greater extent than in any previous year. In that policy it will continue. It is seeking to prevent a condition which would at once destroy all labor unions and all else that is the foundation of civilization by maintaining the authority and sanctity of the law. When that goes all goes. It costs something but it is the cheapest thing that can be bought; it causes some inconvenience but it is the foundation of all convenience, the orderly execution of the laws.

The people understand this thoroughly. They know that the laws are their laws and speak their voice. They know that this Government is their Government founded on their will, administered by their representatives. Disobedience to it is disobedience to the people. They know that the property of the Commonwealth is their property. Destruction of it destroys their substance. The public security is their security. When that is gone they are in deadly peril. And knowing this the people have a determination to support the Government with a resolution that is unchanging.

It is my purpose to maintain the Government of Massachusetts as it was founded by her people, the protector of the rights of all but subservient to none. It is my purpose to maintain unimpaired the authority of her laws, her jurisdiction, her peace, her security. This ancient faith of Massachusetts which became the great faith of America, she reëstablished in her Constitution before the army of Washington had gained our independence, declaring for "a government of laws and not of men." In that faith she still abides. Let him challenge it who dares. All who love Massachusetts, who believe in America, are bound to defend it. The choice lies between living under coercion and intimidation, the forces of evil, or under the laws of the people, orderly, speaking with their settled convictions, the revelation of a divine authority.

XL

WILLIAMS COLLEGE

October 17, 1919

THERE speaks here with the voice of immortality one who loved Massachusetts. On every side arise monuments to that enduring affection bred not of benefits received but of services rendered, of sacrifices made, that the province of Massachusetts Bay might live enlightened and secure. A bit of parchment has filled libraries. A few hundred dollars has enriched generations. The spirit of a single liberty-loving soldier has raised up a host that has shaken the earth with its martial tread, laying low the hills but exalting the valleys. Here Colonel Ephraim Williams still executes his will, still disposes of his patrimony, still leads the soldiers of the free to an enduring victory, and with a power greater than the sword stands guard on the frontier marches of the Commonwealth.

Honor compels that honor be recognized. In compliance with that requirement this day has been set apart by this institution of letters in testimony of the merit of her sons. Nearly one half of her living alumni were under the direct service of the Nation in the great war. Into all branches of the service, civil and military, they went from the alumni, from the class rooms, from the faculty, up to President Garfield himself, who served as Director of the Fuel Administration. From America and her allies has come the highest of recognition, conferred by citation, awards, and decorations. Their individual deeds of valor I shall not relate. They are known to all. Advisedly I say that they have not been surpassed among men. Their heroism was no less heroic because it was unconscious there or because of befitting modesty it is unostentatious here. There was yet a courage unequaled by the most momentous dangers which were met by those now marked with fame and a capacity in the others which would have matched equal events with equal fortitude. In the most grateful recognition of all this, to the living and the dead, by their Alma Mater the Commonwealth of Massachusetts reverently joins.

But this day, if it is truly to represent the spirit of this college, means more than a glorification of the past. It was by a stern determination to discharge the duties of the present that Ephraim Williams provided for a future filled with a glory that must not yet be termed complete. His thoughts were not on himself nor on material things. Had he chosen to inscribe his name upon a monument of granite or of bronze it would have gone the way of all the earth. Enlightening the soul of his fellow man he made his mark which all eternity cannot erase. A soldier, he did not

> "put his trust
> In reeking tube and iron shard"

to save his countrymen, but like Solomon chose first knowledge and wisdom and to his choice has likewise been added a splendor of material prosperity.

Earth's great lesson is written here. In it all men may read the interpretation of the founder of this college, of the meaning of America, of the motive high and true which has inspired her soldiers. Not unmindful of a desire for economic justice but scorning sordid gain, not seeking the spoils of war but a victory of righteousness, they came, subordinating the finite to the infinite, placing their trust in that which does not pass away. This precept heretofore observed must not be abandoned now. A desire for the earth and the fullness thereof must not lure our people from their truer selves. Those who seek for a sign merely in a greatly increased material prosperity, however worthy that may be, disappointed through all the ages, will be disappointed now. Men find their true satisfaction in

something higher, finer, nobler than all
that. We sought no spoils from war; let
us seek no spoil from peace. Let us remember Babylon and Carthage and that city
which her people, flushed with purple pride,
dared call Eternal.

This college and her sons have turned
their eyes resolutely toward the morning.
Above the roar of reeking strife they hear
the voice of the founder. Their actions
have matched their vision. They have seen.
They have heard. They have done. I thank
you for receiving me into their company,
so romantic, so glorious, and for enrolling
me as a soldier in the legion of Colonel
Ephraim Williams.

XLI

CONCERNING TEACHERS' SALARIES

OCTOBER 29, 1919

A Letter to the Mayor of Boston

MY DEAR MR. MAYOR:

It will be with a good deal of satisfaction that I coöperate with you and any other cities of Massachusetts for the purpose of increasing the pay of those engaged in the teaching of the youth of our Commonwealth. It has become notorious that the pay for this most important function is much less than that which prevails in commercial life and business activities.

Roger Ascham, the teacher to Queen Elizabeth, about 1565, in discussing this question, wrote: "And it is pity that commonly more care is had, yea and that among very wise men, to find out rather a cunning man for their horse than a cunning man for their children. They say nay in word, but they do so in deed. For to the one they will gladly give a stipend of two hundred crowns by the year and are loath to offer to the other two hundred shillings. God that sitteth in Heaven laugheth their choice to scorn and rewardeth their liberality as it should. For he suffereth them to have tame and well-ordered horses, but wild and unfortunate children, and therefore in the end they find more pleasure in their horse than comfort in their children."

In an address which I made at a Harvard College Commencement I undertook to direct attention to the inadequate compensation paid to our teachers, whether in the universities, public schools, or the pulpits of the land. It is perfectly clear that more money must be provided for these purposes, which surpass in their importance all our other public activities, both by government appropriation and by private charity.

It is significant that the number of teachers who are in training in our normal schools has decreased in the past twelve or fifteen years from three thousand to two thousand, while the number of students in colleges and technical schools has increased. The people of the Commonwealth cannot support the Government unless the Government supports them.

The condition which was described by the teacher of Queen Elizabeth, that greater compensation is paid for the unimportant things than is paid for training the intellectual abilities of our youth, might exist in the sixteenth century, but it ought not to exist in the twentieth century.

Fortunately for us, the sterling character of teachers of all kinds has kept them at their task even though we have failed to show them due appreciation, and up to the present time the public has suffered little.

But unless a change is made and a new policy adopted, the cause of education will break down. It will either become a trade for those little fitted for it or be abandoned altogether, instead of remaining the noblest profession, which it has been and ought to be.

There are some things that are fundamental. In the sixteenth century the voice of the people was little heard. If the sovereign had wisdom, that might suffice. But in the twentieth century the people are sovereign. What they think determines every question of civilization. Unless they are well trained, well informed, and well instructed, unless a proper value is put on knowledge and wisdom, the value of all material things will be lost.

There is now no pains too great, no cost too high, to prevent or diminish the duty enjoined by the Constitution of the Commonwealth that wisdom and knowledge, as well as virtue, be generally diffused among the body of the people.

This important subject ought to be considered and a remedy provided at the special session of the General Court.

XLII

STATEMENT TO THE PRESS
ELECTION DAY, NOVEMBER 4, 1919

MY thanks are due to the millions of my
fellow citizens of Massachusetts. I offer
them freely, without undertaking to spec-
ify, to all who have supported the great
cause of the supremacy of the law. The
heart of the people has proven again sound
and true. No misrepresentation has blinded
them, no sophistry has turned them. They
have listened to the truth and followed it.
They have again disappointed those who
distrusted them. They have turned away
from those who sought to play upon their
selfishness. They have justified those who
trusted them. They have justified America.

The attempt to appeal to class prejudice
has failed. The men of Massachusetts are
not labor men, or policemen, or union men,
or poor men, or rich men, or any other class

of men first; they are Americans first. The wage-earners have vindicated themselves. They have shown by their votes that they resent trying to use them for private interests, or to employ them to resist the operation of the Government. They are for the Government. They are against those who are against the Government. American institutions are safe in their hands. Some of those who have posed as their leaders and argued that the wage-earners were patriotic because those leaders told them to be may well now inquire whether the case did not stand the other way about. It begins to look as if those who attempt to lead the wage-earners must first show that they themselves are patriotic if they are to have any following. The patriotism of some alleged leaders was not the cause but the effect of the patriotism of the wage-earners.

Three words tell the result. Massachusetts is American. The election will be a welcome demonstration to the Nation and to people everywhere who believe that liberty can only be secured by obedience to law.

XLIII

SPEECH AT TREMONT TEMPLE
SATURDAY, NOVEMBER 1, 1919, 8 P.M

REVELATION has not ceased. The strength of a righteous cause has not grown less. The people of Massachusetts are patriotic before they are partisan, they are not for men but for measures, not for selfishness but for duty, and they will support their Government. Revelation has not ceased and faith in men has not failed. They cannot be intimidated, they cannot be coerced, they cannot be deceived, and their sovereignty is not for sale.

When this campaign is over it will be a rash man who will again attempt to further his selfish interests by dragging a great party name in the mire and seeking to gain the honor of office by trafficking with disorder. The conduct of public affairs is not a game. Responsible office does not go to the crafty. Governments are not founded upon an association for public plunder but on the coöperation of men wherein each is seeking to do his duty.

The past five years have been like an earthquake. They have shaken the institutions of men to their very foundations. It has been a time of searchings and questionings. It has been a time of great awakenings. There has been an overpowering resolution among men to make things better. Despotisms have been falling. Republics have been rising. There has been rebellion everywhere against usurped authority. With all that America has been entirely sympathetic. There has been bred in the blood through generations a great sympathy for all peoples struggling to be free. We have a deep conviction that "resistance to tyranny is obedience to law." And on that conviction we have stood for three centuries. Time and experience have but strengthened our belief that it is sound.

But like all rules of action it only applies to the conditions it describes. All authority is not usurped authority. Any government is not tyranny. These are the counterfeits. There are no counterfeits of the unreal. It is only of the real and true that men seek to pass spurious imitations.

There are among us a great mass of people who have been reared for generations under a government of tyranny and oppression. It is ingrained in their blood that there is no other form of government. They are disposed and inclined to think our institutions partake of the same nature as these they have left behind. We know they are wrong. They must be shown they are wrong.

There is a just government. There are righteous laws. We know the formula by which they are produced. The principle is best stated in the immortal Declaration of Independence to be "the consent of the governed." It is from that source our Gov-

ernment derives its just powers and pro-
mulgates its righteous laws. They are the
will of the people, the settled conviction
derived from orderly deliberation, that take
on the sanctity ascribed to the people's
voice. Along with the binding obligation to
resist tyranny goes the other admonition,
that "obedience to law is liberty," — such
law and so derived.

These principles, which I have but
lightly sketched, are the foundation of
American institutions, the source of American freedom and the faith of any party entitled to call itself American. It constitutes
truly the rule of the people. It justifies and
sanctifies the authority of our laws and the
obligation to support our Government. It
is democracy administered through repre-
sentation.

There are only two other choices, anarchy or despotism — Russia, present and
past. For the most part human existence
has been under the one or the other of

these. Both have failed to minister to the highest welfare of the people. Unless American institutions can provide for that welfare the cause of humanity is hopeless. Unless the blessings of prosperity, the rewards of industry, justice and liberty, the satisfaction of duty well done, can come under a rule of the people, they cannot come at all. We may as well abandon hope and, yielding to the demands of selfishness, each take what he can.

We had hoped these questions were settled. But nothing is settled that evil and selfish men can find advantage for themselves in overthrowing. We must eternally smite the rock of public conscience if the waters of patriotism are to pour forth. We must ever be ready to point out the success of our country as justification of our determination to support it.

No one can deny that we are in the midst of an abounding prosperity. No one can deny that this prosperity is well distributed; especially is this true of the wage-earner. Industrially, commercially, financially, America has been a success. The wealth of Massachusetts is increasing rapidly. There are large deposits going into her savings institutions, during banking hours with each tick of the clock more than $12.50, with each minute more than $750, with each day over $270,000. Wages and hours of labor were never so favorable. We have attained a standard of living among our people the like of which never before existed on earth.

Intellectually our progress compares with our prosperity. The opportunity for education is not only large, but it is well used. The school is everywhere. Ignorance is a disgrace. The turrets of college and university dot the land. Their student bodies were never so large. Science and invention, literature and art flourish.

There is higher standard of justice in all the affairs of life than in the past. Our

commercial transactions are on a higher
plane. There is a moral standard that runs
through all the avenues of our life that has
lifted it into a new position and gives to
men a keener sense of honor in all things.
There has come to be a new realization of
the brotherhood of man, a new significance
to religion. The war aroused a new patriotism, and revealed the strength of our
moral power.

The issue in Massachusetts is whether
these conditions can endure. Will men realize their blessing and exhibit the resolution
to support and defend the foundation on
which they rest? Having saved Europe are
we ready to surrender America? Having
beaten the foe from without are we to fall a
victim to the foe from within?

All of this is put in question by the issue
of this campaign. That one fundamental issue is the support of the Government in its
determination to maintain order. On that
all of these opportunities depend.

There can be no material prosperity without order. Stores and banks could not open. Factories could not run, railways could not operate. What was the value of plate glass and goods, the value of real estate in Boston at three o'clock, A.M., September 10? Unless the people vote to sustain order that value is gone entirely. Business is ended.

On order depends all intellectual progress. Without it all schools close, libraries are empty, education stops. Disorder was the forerunner of the Dark Ages.

Without order the moral progress of the people would be lost. With the schools would go the churches. There could be no assemblages for worship, no services even for the departed, piety would be swallowed up in viciousness.

I have understated the result of disorder. Man has not the imagination, the ability to overstate it. There are those who aim to bring about exactly this result. I propose at all times to resist them with all the power at the command of the Chief Executive of Massachusetts.

Naturally the question arises, what shall we do to defend our birthright? In the first place everybody must take a more active part in public affairs. It will not do for men to send, they must go. It is not enough to draw a check. Good government cannot be bought, it has to be given. Office has great opportunities for doing wrong, but equal chance for doing right. Unless good citizens hold office bad citizens will. People see the office-holder rather than the Government. Let the worth of the office-holder speak the worth of the government. The voice of the people speaks by the voice of the individual. Duty is not collective, it is personal. Let every inhabitant make known his determination to support law and order. That duty is supreme.

That the supremacy of the law, the preservation of the Government itself by the maintenance of order, should be the issue of this campaign was entirely due to circumstances beyond my control. That any one should dare to put in jeopardy the stability of our Government for the purpose of securing office was to me inconceivable. That any one should attempt to substitute the will of any outside organization for the authority conferred by law upon the representatives of the people had never occurred to me. But the issue arose by action of some of the police of Boston and it was my duty to meet it. I shall continue to administer the law of all the people.

I should have been pleased to make this campaign on the record of the past year. I should have been pleased to show what the march of progress had been under the people's government, what action had been taken for the relief of those who toil with their hands as well as their heads,—and the record was never more alluring,—what has been done to advance the business and commercial interests of this great industrial Commonwealth, what has promoted public health, what has assisted in agricultural development, the progress made in providing transportation, the increased opportunity given our youth for education. In particular I should have desired to point out the great pride Massachusetts has in her war record and the abundant way she has shown her gratitude for her service men and women, surpassing every other State. All this is a record not of promises, but of achievement. It is one in which the voters of the Commonwealth may well take a deep satisfaction. It is there, it stands, it cannot be argued away. No deception can pervert it. It endures.

All these are the result of ordered liberty — the result of living under the law. It is the great desire of Massachusetts to continue such legislation of progress and humanity. Those who are attempting to wrench the scepter of authority from the representatives of the people, to subvert the jurisdiction of her laws, are the enemies not only of progress, but of all present achievement, not only of what we hope for, but of what we have.

This is the cause of all the people, especially of the weak and defenseless. Their only refuge is the protection of the law. The people have come to understand this. They are taking the deciding of this election into their own hands regardless of party. If the people win who can lose? They are awake to the words of Daniel Webster, "nothing will ruin the country if the people themselves will undertake its safety; and nothing can save it if they leave that safety in any hands but their own."

My fellow citizens of Massachusetts, to you I commend this cause. To you who have added the glory of the hills and plains of France to the glory of Concord and Bunker Hill, to you who have led when others faltered, to you again is given the leadership. Grasp it. Secure it. Make it decisive. Make the discharge of the great trust you now hold an example of hope for righteousness everywhere, a new guaranty that the Government of America shall endure.

𝕮𝖍𝖊 𝕽𝖎𝖛𝖊𝖗𝖘𝖎𝖉𝖊 𝕻𝖗𝖊𝖘𝖘

CAMBRIDGE . MASSACHUSETTS

U . S . A